EVERYTHING ANCIENT
WAS ONCE NEW

INDIGENOUS PACIFICS
SERIES EDITORS

*Noelani Goodyear-Kaʻōpua
and April K. Henderson*

*FACING THE SPEARS OF CHANGE: THE LIFE
AND LEGACY OF JOHN PAPA ʻĪʻĪ*
Marie Alohalani Brown

*FOUND IN TRANSLATION: MANY MEANINGS
ON A NORTH AUSTRALIAN MISSION*
Laura Rademaker

*THE PAST BEFORE US:
MOʻOKŪʻAUHAU AS METHODOLOGY*
edited by Nālani Wilson-Hokowhitu

EVERYTHING ANCIENT
WAS ONCE NEW

Indigenous Persistence from Hawai'i to Kahiki

EMALANI CASE

UNIVERSITY OF HAWAI'I PRESS
HONOLULU

26 25 24 23 22 21   6 5 4 3 2 1

Library of Congress Cataloging-in-Publication Data

Names: Case, Emalani, author.
Title: Everything ancient was once new : indigenous persistence from
Hawai'i to Kahiki / Emalani Case.
Other titles: Indigenous Pacifics.
Description: Honolulu : University of Hawai'i Press, [2021] | Series:
Indigenous Pacifics | Includes bibliographical references and index.
Identifiers: LCCN 2020051234 | ISBN 9780824886806 (cloth) | ISBN
9780824886813 (paperback) | ISBN 9780824888183 (pdf) | ISBN
9780824888206 (epub) | ISBN 9780824888190 (kindle edition)
Subjects: LCSH: Hawaiians—Ethnic identity. | Hawaiians—Social life and
customs. | Indigenous peoples—Oceania—Ethnic identity. |
Hawaii—Social life and customs.
Classification: LCC DU624.65 .C37 2021 | DDC 996/.004—dc23
LC record available at https://lccn.loc.gov/2020051234dh

Cover Art: Ancientness Emerging was created by Keōmailani and Auli'i Case. In their words,
"It depicts wai and 'āina, two ancient and natural features that lash together the very essence
of who we are. Engrained in the pores of life, etched in stone, and emerging from rhythms
set forth by reflection, we take on the strength of our surroundings, our pillars."

This book is dedicated to all aloha ʻāina,
past, present, and future.

Everything Ancient Was Once New

Everything ancient was once new:
a new altar built stone by stone,
each one chosen, collected,
each one passed hand by hand,
stacked together to bear the weight of prayers
thousands and thousands of prayers.

Sweat from palms seeped into pores of stones,
carrying the salt of our bodies, our tears,
to a time we haven't arrived at yet,
a time we are now preparing for,
dreaming into existence with radical hope,
with cries and calls for aloha 'āina.

New altars should be allowed to wear age
in weathered groves, in hoʻokupu,
in stories created and kept safe in pockets
like dried ocean turned to salt,
carrying the promise of the sea
and our inability to be stagnant.

Everything ancient was once new:
a new hale built post by post,
each one positioned upright,
grounded in mountain soils,
standing to shoulder the weight of a nation
thousands and thousands sheltered.

Each lashing drew together strands
like genealogies twisting, forming,
growing and birthing new kiaʻi
for a time we haven't arrived at yet,
a time we build pebble by pebble,
facing the future with our backs.

New shelters should be allowed to wear age
in dried leaves and weathered woods,
in songs and chants sung, lashed together
like aloha 'āina linked in arms to guard mountains,
standing with generations forward and back
and our refusal to remain idle.

Last night our new was denied ancientness,
our descendants denied the right
to collect our prayers from altars
to find shelter for awakening,
to find salt for healing
kept safe for them in grooves.

Last night our new was denied ancientness,
dismantled in the dark, destroyed:
an altar taken apart stone by stone,
a hale disassembled lashing by lashing,
posts pulled up from the earth in fear
of our ferocious love of place.

Everything ancient was once new.
Our structures were denied age.
But no amount of dismantling, disassembling,
desecrating or disrespecting of our right to be
can deny us our ancientness,
our ability to stand with thousands and thousands.

There can be no taking apart of this moʻokūʻauhau,
no separating us from the kūpuna we carry
in our bones, in our skin, in the salt we cry.
You can take an altar, pull up the posts of a hale,
you can even do it in the dark, hiding.
But as long as we are here, you cannot deny us

and our right to time.

    —Emalani Case

CONTENTS

Preface

The events that inspired portions of this book, and that will appear in the chapters ahead, took place in the latter half of 2019. From July to November of that year, I moved to and from different movements both to protect place—as in the movement to protect Mauna Kea in Hawaiʻi and to protect Ihumātao in Aotearoa—and to stand for Indigenous persistence. This book was therefore written to highlight these few months and to capture how engagement in these various events and movements transformed the way I thought about—and continue to think about—the central concept of this work: Kahiki. I wanted to bring this concept, whose life often seems to speak more to the past than it does to the present, to the *now* so that I could argue for its continued relevance in Hawaiian lives today. It is not only a term that speaks to our origins or to our awareness of the outside world but also a concept that can carry new functions as we continue to persist as Indigenous peoples.

Producing this book in this way gave me the opportunity to put into action what I was writing about, or to think about the role, function, and importance of a concept such as Kahiki in contemporary times, spaces, and actions. It allowed me to actually use Kahiki in the ways I was proposing it be used: to understand and articulate what I was experiencing, to unpack what was unfolding around me, and to create and maintain spaces for continuing to do the hard work of addressing the present so that we can adjust our lives and realities to match the futures we dream of. While for me the events that allowed this learning occurred in the span of a few months, their significance will have life far beyond this time as they show us how we might use ancient concepts and continually make them new for changing times. My hope, therefore, is that anyone who engages with this work be able to pick it up, consider the ideas presented, and add to them, challenge them, change them, and give them new functions. This is how our concepts will survive, and this is how we, as Indigenous peoples, will persist.

Acknowledgments

One of my favorite poems is Maya Angelou's "Our Grandmothers." In it, the incredible Angelou states, "I go forth/alone and stand as ten thousand."[1] As Indigenous peoples, we know we take our ancestors with us wherever we go. We know we carry them in our bones and in our blood in the same way that our descendants will carry us. We know we never stand alone, and that our children and grandchildren will never stand alone either. Therefore, while I put the words of this book to the pages that follow, I cannot take full credit for what those words say. I will own the mistakes and shortcomings myself. The moments of inspiration, however, belong to those who inspired them: my ancestors, my fellow aloha 'āina (all ancestors in becoming), and those who haven't been born yet, those who feed my every hope and dream. This was created by, and for, all of us.

To name just a few of the ten thousand who were instrumental in the writing of this book, and to give them proper acknowledgment, I'd like to write out their names and give them each my deepest appreciation.

To Teresia Teaiwa, the fierce and fiery canoe, I could not have explored the depths of Kahiki without you. It was with you that I first set sail on this journey, and it is with your memory and your teachings that I continue to navigate this world of Pacific studies in your wake.

To Pua Case, my Bonnie, thank you for first introducing me to Kahiki in dance and story. One of my greatest honors in life is being able to call you my cousin and my teacher. You are the epitome of what it means to be a Kanaka Maoli woman today, and I can only hope to be a lālā that resembles you, my lifelong kumu. I love you beyond words.

To all of the kiaʻi who inspired significant parts of this book, from Mauna Kea to Ihumātao, thank you for tending to the ʻāina and to the whenua as you do, as our ancestors did, and as our future generations will continue to do.

To my dear hoa, Kawika Aipa, thank you for ensuring that I did not become so consumed by the writing of this book that I could not still get out and see the sky. This windy city would not be the same without you, my "other Hawaiian."

To my colleagues and students at Vaʻaomanū Pasifika, it is an honor to be on this vaka with you. I look forward to all of our journeys ahead.

To two academic powerhouses I admire greatly, April K. Henderson and Noelani Goodyear-Kaʻōpua, thank you for giving me the chance to share this work with the world and to be part of Indigenous Pacifics.

To the kālai waʻa who have been inspiring me since I was a little girl, thank you for letting me record your stories. I know they will continue to guide my work for years to come.

To every artist, activist, intellectual, leader, healer, poet, and radical thinker whose words appear in this book, thank you for every way your voices have inspired my own.

Lastly, to my parents, my siblings, and all my nieces and nephews, I love you beyond love. To my brothers, Kanaina, Hawaiian, and Kauka, thank you for being my pillars, for showing me how to stand in the world, and for letting me follow my dreams even when they take me away. To my sisters, Keōmailani and Auliʻi, I'm thankful every day that we were born both as sisters and as friends. Having your artwork on the cover of this book is one of my deepest joys. This work is all of us, together, as we always will be. To my dad, thank you for teaching me aloha ʻāina. You showed me how to love ʻāina fiercely, and it is because of you that I know how to love and nourish my home from wherever I happen to be in the world. Writing about aloha ʻāina was possible only because of every way you've embodied it. Finally, to my mom, no one has taught me more about radical hope than you have. Thank you for every time your belief and confidence in me, and your hope and love for me, superseded anything I could give myself. Every single thing I accomplish in life will be because of the hope you gifted me at birth, the hope you nurture every day, and the hope you have inspired me to have for myself, for our people, for our ʻāina, and for the world.

No work on Indigeneity would be possible without the lands, waters, and oceans that nourish and ground us. I have been blessed to live in two places that both fill me and give me reasons to stand. From the windswept hillsides of Waimea, Hawai'i, to the flowing streams of Te-Whanganui-a-Tara, Aotearoa, I walk as an Indigenous woman because you give me space to breathe and the motivation to make each and every breath sovereign.

INTRODUCTION

Let Me Be Your Sanctuary

The farthest horizons of our hopes and fears are cobbled by our poems, carved from the rock experiences of our daily lives. As they become known to and accepted by us, our feelings and the honest exploration of them become sanctuaries and spawning grounds for the most radical and daring of ideas.

—*Audre Lorde, Sister Outsider*

Standing before a group of kiaʻi (protectors) for Mauna Kea, I shivered in the cold, weighted with layers of clothing, a bundle of ideas, and the pressure to share some of them.[1] I had been asked to say a few words, to offer a bit of inspiration or knowledge for those gathered. I felt both inadequate and inspired. It was the kind of moment where you're certain someone else should be filling the role, but also confident that there are words that need to be shared and that maybe, just maybe, you're the one to share them. The day before, I had sat on a bed of smooth pāhoehoe (a type of lava), a journal propped on my knee, the mauna (mountain) in my sight, and written about

sanctuary. Beginning a poem, I scribbled, "Let me be your sanctuary/a place
to find comfort when your soils have been dispersed/roots unearthed, left
hanging." I didn't fully understand these words, carved from the lava beneath
me, until I stood there, adorned in mist and my brother's heavy camou-
flage jacket, the mauna cloaked in clouds, a group of kiaʻi listening, and the
words finding shape and meaning as they came out of my mouth. As those
words took shape, unconsciously, so did this book. That moment and that
poem became the spawning ground for the "radical and daring" hope that is
Everything Ancient Was Once New.

The kiaʻi and I had gathered and taken our position on the Mauna Kea
Access Road as we had been doing for days, and as kiaʻi are still doing as I
write this, determined to halt the construction of the proposed and highly
controversial Thirty Meter Telescope (TMT) on our mountain (a story and
an issue that will appear at different points, and in different ways, throughout this book).[2] Days prior, thirty-three kūpuna (elders) had been arrested
for protecting Mauna Kea.[3] When I arrived, two days after the arrests were
made, the atmosphere was still tense, still uncertain, but also hopeful. What
was created at the base of the mountain, on a road surrounded by lava fields,
was a place of awakening, a place of rising. It was, as had been declared the
weekend before my arrival at the mountain, a puʻuhonua: a sanctuary, a place
of safety and refuge. People came from all over the pae ʻāina (the archipelago), wanting to be *at* and *with* the mountain, wanting to support the growing movement, and, I suspect for many, wanting to be in a place where they
could find comfort in standing for something larger than themselves. I was
there because the mauna brought me home, back to the base of a mountain I
grew up with and around. It pulled me to purchase a plane ticket, to fly back
to my ʻāina (land) from Aotearoa, where I live and work, to find sanctuary
in my place, my mountain, my people, and our never-ending commitment
to aloha ʻāina (love of place).

The words I spoke that morning, standing before the kiaʻi, came to inspire the direction of this book. Though portions of the book are informed
by my PhD research and thesis, it was that moment, standing there in the
cold, that made me pause and consider how early drafts of this book needed
to shift to meet the times and, perhaps more importantly, to meet my engagements *in* these times. In months prior, revisions of my book had been
slow. The first manuscript I produced reflected who, where, and what I was
then, as a PhD student working on a thesis back in 2014. It also, if I am being
honest, did more to trace the life of concepts and ideas in the past than add
to them, extend them, or give them new life and meaning for the future. As
I read through drafts and attempted to update them, I realized that I needed
to tap into who, where, and what I am *now*, and that I had the opportunity,
and perhaps even the responsibility, to provide new/renewed concepts, to be
ready to tackle the issues of our current and shifting worlds. Going home to

the mauna reminded me of this. While I am not drastically different from who I was when I completed my degree in 2015, I know that I've changed, that our worlds have changed, that I have grown, that my passion for our lands, waters, and seas has deepened (even when I didn't think it could), and that my book needs to reflect these changes.

My PhD research focused on one central concept: Kahiki. Kahiki is at once an ancestral homeland for Hawaiians and the knowledge that there is life to be found beyond our shores. It is where we say our ancestors came from when they boarded double-hulled canoes in other parts of Oceania and set sail to discover new homes. Kahiki is therefore both a symbol of ancestral connection and the potential that comes with remembering and acting upon that connection. What I realized that morning, at the base of our mauna, is that Kahiki is also, and has always been, a sanctuary. When I began speaking, a friend of mine pulled her phone out and recorded my brief talk. Though I didn't know she was filming, I was later thankful. When she shared the video with me, I watched it back and heard, from my own lips, the words that would inspire my revisions, my rewriting, and eventually the publication of this work: "When I think about our kūpuna, they're my puʻuhonua. They're the place that you can always think about. Puʻuhonua, to me, doesn't always have to be physical. Sometimes it's cultural. It's psychological. It's what can you think of, *who* can you think of, that is going to encourage you to stand stronger, to rise taller, to be braver than you ever thought you could be." In the years that I spent thinking about Kahiki, sitting with and in Kahiki, carrying the memory of it with me in my travels and migrations, I realized it was the place—the nonphysical place of deep meaning—that I found refuge in. It was where I could recall lessons from my kūpuna; where I could remember their strength and their agency; where I could find inspiration in their shifting articulations of self and nationhood; and where I could source encouragement to keep thinking, creating, and shaping our worlds today and every day. However, as sanctuaries also provide space and time for deep, critical reflection, it was also where I could go to challenge myself, to critique my own complacency, to put myself in check, and to find areas of discomfort necessary for growth. This book is a result of my many varied visits to Kahiki as a place to take pause, to find perspective, to (re)orient myself, to examine our worlds, and to gather what is necessary to meet the needs of today.

In the chapters that follow, I will therefore visit Kahiki as a sanctuary as it was, as it is, and, hopefully, as it can be. In doing so, I will propose and argue for reactivated and reinvigorated engagements with Kahiki, giving it, in each chapter, new/renewed functions for contemporary times. My hope is that in visiting this place of meaning and finding the lessons it holds and the opportunities it provides, I may offer ways to propel and support some of our movements to protect land and water, to work toward decolonizing our physical and ideological spaces, and to reconnect to other peoples and places in our Pacific in ways that are purposeful and meaningful. To do so, I will trace Kahiki as a concept through pivotal moments in history and in contemporary events, explaining that even while not always referenced by name, the idea of Kahiki was, and is, always present and always full of potential. I will also explore Kahiki in new ways and new contexts so that in the process of constantly renewing it I can simultaneously ensure that it will continue to grow and age, solidifying its place as another ancient concept and tool not only for remembering the past but also for acting in the present and far into the future.

From Hawai'i to Kahiki

Since Kahiki ultimately refers to space outside of Hawai'i, this book will inevitably engage with other places and peoples and will strive to offer ideas that may find relevance in larger conversations about Indigeneity; renaissance and cultural revival; colonialism, settler colonialism, and decolonization; social and environmental justice; and even the urgent worldwide need for hopes and dreams. In saying this, though, I must be upfront about my positionality and about both the potentials and limits of this book. I am a Kanaka Maoli woman,[4] a teacher of Pacific studies, and a writer and academic whose experiences in the Pacific have largely taken place between two settler colonies: Hawai'i and Aotearoa. Therefore, what I will present will undoubtedly be centered in Hawai'i and in distinctly Hawaiian concepts, and will largely involve conversations about issues that are most pressing and pertinent in the settler colonial Pacific. While incorporating work from a range of disciplines, experiences, locations, and colonial realities, my aim is to speak to the particularities of our situation in Hawai'i, to the parallels (or disjunctures) between our concerns and those of other nations in our region, and further, to the positions and positionings of Indigenous peoples around the world.[5] (In doing so, I will also unpack the term "Indigenous," particularly in chapters 2 and 5, recognizing both its opportunities and its limitations in the Pacific.)

The particular aims, themes, and issues guiding this book, I realize, may inadvertently leave people out, and as a result, my engagements with Oceania may be partial and inadequate. As vast and varied as the Pacific is, I know I cannot speak of everyone in the region. Therefore, I admit here that my work focuses more on settler colonies (and therefore those islanders who identify as Indigenous) than it does on the independent Pacific. It also pays far more attention to the Anglophone Pacific than it does to the Francophone, Hispanophone, or Sinophone Pacifics. These are limits that I recognize, and therefore I do not present this work as one that will speak to or for the entire region but rather one that will use the specificities of our concepts, histories, and ways of knowing in Hawai'i to reach out to other places both in the Pacific and around the world.

As a teacher and scholar in Pacific studies, I endeavor to create work that is interdisciplinary, that involves comparative analysis, and that accounts for Indigenous ways of knowing. These are the key tenets of Pacific studies that were outlined by the late Teresia Teaiwa, my PhD supervisor and friend, and are prescriptions I now teach my students.[6] Acknowledging my base in Pacific studies, I also try to locate my work at the intersections between Pacific studies, Hawaiian studies, and Indigenous studies, hoping that being positioned in the tensions and convergences between them will be generative. While my work is unabashedly centered in Hawai'i, as that is quite simply the center of everything I am, it uses Kahiki to look outward, to remember and activate connections, and to expand a Kanaka Maoli sense of obligation beyond the shores of our home. Thus, while it is nationalistic, it is also regional and global. My goal in each chapter is to visit Kahiki in order to give it new and renewed function as a concept in contemporary times. While it is not my aim to propose that *all* people use Kahiki as a concept, I hope that it will inspire Kānaka Maoli to do so, to draw on the wisdom of their ancestors and to add to that wisdom for the future. At the same time, I hope that in highlighting one of our concepts that other peoples will be motivated to do the same with their own unique ways of knowing, doing, and orienting in the world.

Kahiki

I first encountered Kahiki in dance and story. When I was just a baby, my first cousin, Pua Case, a kumu hula (hula teacher) and a staunch leader in the effort to protect Mauna Kea, made the conscious choice to take me as her student. Therefore, at a young age, I spent days and sometimes weeks with her, sitting at her side, listening to her sing and chant, watching her as she worked with her older students, mesmerized by her movements. When I was old enough to begin my formal training, I was introduced not only to the basics of hula—or to basic foot and hand motions and the principles of discipline and how to hold your body—but also to the stories that my motions would tell. While some dances and chants honored our chiefs, or told the history of specific places in Hawai'i, others told epic tales of migration, recounting the journeys that some of our gods and goddesses, heroes and heroines, chiefs and chiefesses made from Kahiki to Hawai'i. Thus, as a little girl, Kahiki was a place of departure, a place that people left in their search for something more, or something else, in our sea of islands.[7] It was, quite simply, where our ancestors came from. I never questioned it, never doubted its place in our genealogies, never denied its importance. However, as I grew older and realized that its meaning shifted and that its nature changed (and could even *be* changed) over time, I realized the value of tracking those changes to see what they could reveal about the people who made them, and further, about our ability to do the same.

Valerio Valeri describes Kahiki as "the invisible place . . . out of which come the gods, ancestors, regalia, edible plants, and ritual institutions—the life of the Hawaiians and the means to reproduce it."[8] However, as I have come to understand, it is not so much that Kahiki is "invisible" as it is fluid and unrestrained, much like the ocean in which it originates. In fact, Kahiki is indeed visible in what it has produced and what it continues to produce. As Kānaka Maoli, for instance, we are products of Kahiki. There are many stories of travel between Kahiki and Hawaiʻi. Thus, it is a place. However, it is not bound to a specific location. Rather, it is the general understanding that life in the form of people, ideas, and sources of sustenance—be it physical, spiritual, intellectual, or cultural—may have originated elsewhere in the Pacific before coming to our islands aboard double-hulled canoes. Therefore, Kahiki could refer to Tahiti, as will be explained further in chapter 1. However, it could also refer to the Marquesas, to the Cook Islands, to Sāmoa, to Fiji, or to any other islands that our peoples may have come from in the Pacific.

Encapsulated in this one term, "Kahiki," are our ancestral memories of migration. When islanders traveled to different parts of the Pacific region, they maintained knowledge of their homelands. According to Greg Dening, as people moved, "each generation had passed on to the next generation the knowledge, experience, and wisdom with which they had imprinted their human spirit on their landscapes and seascapes. This was the Homeland to which a first people would look back after their next step."[9] Although the names of these homelands differ throughout the Pacific, the concept is similar: islanders knew that their life in a particular group of islands was dependent on other places and peoples that, no matter how distant, remained an integral part of them. After generations, "although memories of real homelands and ancestors inevitably faded," as Peter Adds argues, "their importance was not reduced, even if the details changed."[10] When the specificity of these "homelands" was blurred, one name came to represent the genealogical connections that people shared with other places in the Pacific. What was Pulotu for some, therefore, became Hawaiki for others.[11] For my ancestors in Hawaiʻi, this was Kahiki. It was and is the homeland we continue to look back to.

In his book *Return to Kahiki: Native Hawaiians in Oceania*, Kealani Cook talks about how when voyaging to islands south of Hawaiʻi ceased, tales of Kahiki may have taken on "mythic" qualities. Despite some of these tales' fantastical elements and the blurring of specifics, however, "Kahiki remains a place of significant mana."[12] It is a place of power that continues to remind Kānaka Maoli of our ancestral connections to the rest of the Pacific. As an ʻōlelo noʻeau, or a Hawaiian proverb, states, "Aia ke ola i Kahiki," "Life is in Kahiki."[13] While the mythic qualities of some of our Kahiki narratives have led to their being disregarded and disrespected, especially in academic circles, Kahiki, at its core, is the knowledge that our life in Hawaiʻi is intimately linked to the life of other islands and islanders that, although out of sight, are never out of memory. This connection is not mythic; it is not fantastical. It is real, embodied, and enacted.

Though beginning as an ancestral homeland, however, Kahiki eventually took on new meaning as Kanaka engagements with the outside world expanded. In his book *The World and All the Things upon It: Native Hawaiian Geographies of Exploration*, David A. Chang talks about the importance of names like Kahiki in resisting the often-assumed fallacy "that it was Captain Cook in 1778 that introduced Kānaka to the idea that a world beyond their shores existed."[14] As recorded in countless chants, prayers, proverbs, and stories, Kānaka Maoli knew of lands and peoples beyond their shores.[15] When Europeans such as Cook first came to Hawaiʻi, they were seen as coming from afar. Thus, Kahiki as a concept was stretched to accommodate *all* places, not just those that our migrating ancestors initially traveled from. The work of both Chang and Cook is critical in tracing engagements with and understandings of Kahiki. Cook explores connections with Oceania that were recalled and enacted upon in the period between 1850 and 1907, while Chang examines Kanaka explorations of the outside world, even beyond the Pacific, in the nineteenth century. As will be explored in chapter 3 of this book, while Hawaiians traveled outward and made meaning of new and renewed relationships, Kahiki as a concept also shifted for those who remained in Hawaiʻi. It took on new political importance in the nineteenth century, for instance, when threats to Hawaiian sovereignty forced Kānaka into new discussions and debates about nationhood and the place of Kahiki—whether the Pacific or the wider world—in their futures. As Cook emphasizes in his work, perceptions of Kahiki were not always positive, especially if/when Kānaka Maoli began to see their pasts as dark and unenlightened, and their ancestors as ignorant. These views, often promoted in missionary rhetoric, worked to distance Hawaiians not only from their own pasts but from their ancestral connections across the region as well. As Cook explains, "Those most eager to turn their back on Ka Wā ʻŌiwi Wale [precontact Hawaiʻi] were also the most likely to dismiss, condemn, and separate themselves from other islanders as part of that past."[16] They were the most likely, in other words, to see in their Pacific relations what they believed their people used to be: uncivilized, pagan, and in need of saving.

While Kahiki is an opportunity for Kānaka Maoli to remember and activate their Pacific connections—whether to support one another, to work together for the betterment of the region, or to even attempt to decentralize colonial empires in order to recentralize genealogies—it is critical that we are aware of some of the existing and residual perceptions that have been built up over time. Some of the negative views Cook speaks about, for instance, can still be seen carried in our actions and heard in our statements about each other today. In Hawaiʻi, for instance, a concept like Kahiki can be used strategically to honor figures such as Pius Mau Piailug, affectionately known as "Papa Mau"—a master navigator from Satawal in the Caroline Islands, Micronesia, who was pivotal in the revival of noninstrument navigation and wayfinding in Hawaiʻi—while also being strategically distanced when speaking about the influx of Micronesians to Hawaiʻi since the mid 1980s. In the first case, as will be explored in chapter 4, remembering Kahiki can justify the use of Satawalese techniques in "Hawaiian" navigation. In the second case, as will be looked at in chapter 1, forgetting Kahiki can lead to the neglect of genealogical obligations to each other, whether the responsibility of Kānaka Maoli to care for their older Pacific relatives or the responsibility of islanders from Micronesia to understand that Hawaiʻi's settler colonial context can make hosting others, even family, difficult. Forgetting or ignoring Kahiki connections, rather than facing the difficulties of them, has led to racial tensions, prejudices, and in some cases harm.[17] Thus, it is imperative that any examination of Kahiki not get lost in romanticized remembrances of the past but dig into the complexities of the present so that we can repair strained relationships and nurture renewed ones. This is where Kahiki can be both a sanctuary for finding strength and hope as well as a sanctuary for deep, critical reflection, for forgiveness, and for readying oneself to reenter society. Kahiki cannot be called upon only as it supports our agendas, in other words. It must also be remembered even when recalling it is uncomfortable or inconvenient. The chapters of this book will seek to illuminate spaces of both comfort and discomfort in order to highlight the true potential of Kahiki as a sanctuary to visit when necessary for both rejuvenation and serious reminding and reparation.

Sanctuary

When I stood to give my brief speech before the kiaʻi gathered at the base of Mauna Kea, I stood in a puʻuhonua, a sanctuary. Days prior, on the morning of Saturday, July 13, 2019, the Royal Order of Kamehameha I—a society created in 1865 by Lot Kapuāiwa Kamehameha V to honor his grandfather, the great chief Kamehameha I—designated Puʻu Huluhulu a sanctuary in collaboration with protectors of the mountain.[18] A press release issued by the Hawaiian Unity and Liberation Institute (HULI) the day before read, "During times of strife and contention, a Puʻuhonua was a place, or person, that would provide safety, refuge and protection."[19] Coming together at sunrise, the Royal Order, along with kiaʻi, established a sanctuary at Puʻu

Huluhulu to "ensure the safety of all people gathering to protect Maunakea from further desecration and destruction by the proposed Thirty Meter Telescope."[20] This was in response to governor David Ige's announcement that construction would begin the following Monday, July 15, 2019, and that law enforcement officers and members of the National Guard would be mobilized to ensure that construction could commence. Since its designation, Puʻuhonua o Puʻuhuluhulu has become a place of safety for kiaʻi of every background, Kānaka Maoli and non-Hawaiians included. It has become a place of gathering, a place of prayer and ceremony, a place of learning and sharing, and a place of recommitting to the protection of not just the mauna but of all lands and waters. It has become a place where the values of kapu aloha (a commitment to nonviolent direct action) and aloha ʻāina (a fierce love of place) have not only guided those present at the sanctuary but have also permeated surrounding communities and even other nations around the world.

When I spoke that morning, I commented on how Puʻu Huluhulu could become a sanctuary for other Indigenous peoples, a place they could think of when they needed reassurance and strength in their own struggles. People could look to our insistence on acting with aloha, for instance, and our commitment to being led by our kūpuna, and find motivation or inspiration there. I should be clear, however, that my statement was not to suggest that our puʻuhonua be *the* place of refuge for all peoples, or that it even be *the* example for all to follow. Our puʻuhonua has grown and evolved with the movement, adjusting when and where necessary. Therefore, my words were meant to propose that we be sanctuaries for each other, or reminders that there are peoples around the world engaged in similar movements to protect land, space, and the right to be Indigenous *in* those spaces. It was to acknowledge that while we could be a source of strength or comfort for others, that we too would need to look out beyond our shores to witness the rising of other peoples and to be reminded that our efforts were about something so much larger than our individual nations.

That evening, after speaking about sanctuary earlier in the day, I heard news that protectors of Ihumātao, a culturally significant and sacred site in Auckland, New Zealand, were issued an eviction notice. Since 2016, members of Save Our Unique Landscape (SOUL)—made up of residents from the area, mana whenua (those with rights in that particular area), and other supporters—had been occupying Ihumātao to protect it from Fletcher Building Limited's plan to build 480 high-cost homes. When news of the eviction spread on the mauna the next morning, I was asked to write a statement of solidarity to be offered on behalf of the kūpuna and kiaʻi gathered. In the same notebook that I had scribbled in days before, reflecting on sanctuary, I quickly drafted a statement to be read from the puʻuhonua. "From our mauna, Mauna Kea, to your whenua (land) at Ihumātao, we are with you,"

I wrote. Before reading the statement to those gathered, I talked about the incredible amount of love and support coming to the mauna from Māori and others in Aotearoa in the form of prayers, songs, fundraising efforts, educational evenings, and rallies. While we were gathered to protect our mountain, we felt it was important to return our love and support to them, recognizing that although we were in different places, the base of our fights were the same. We were Indigenous peoples saying "not one more": "not one more acre" and "not one more telescope."[21] In the exchange, I realized the true ability of peoples to find sanctuary in each other. Though united in the struggle for our mauna—in the ongoing fight to be heard and respected, to have our beliefs valued and acknowledged, and to keep our lands and waters safe for the future—there was comfort in knowing that we were not alone in our stand. Additionally, when I personally heard about Ihumātao, I felt an even greater responsibility to stand as a kiaʻi, knowing that no matter where I was in the world, I had to align myself with actions and efforts aimed at protecting land and water everywhere. These movements, I realized, were not about us as individuals but about securing a future for our descendants, a future where they can live healthy lives connected to ʻāina, where they can know their whenua as ancestor, and where they can be confident and comfortable living the way their ancestors had taught them to live: as kiaʻi or kaitiaki (guardians).

As mentioned previously, however, the purpose of a sanctuary is not just to offer a place of comfort or encouragement. Sometimes it is a place to reflect deeply, to learn, to cleanse, and to prepare oneself to reenter society. In his serial account "Ka Moolelo Hawaii," published in the Hawaiian-language newspaper *Ke Au Okoa*, noted Kanaka Maoli scholar Samuel Kamakau explains that both people and places could be puʻuhonua. An area of sanctuary could be established as a place to escape death or punishment. Similarly, a high chief could also be a sanctuary, or someone who could pardon others, issuing forgiveness.[22] In this sense, a puʻuhonua could be a place of safety for someone who broke a law or wanted to escape punishment or death. Reentering society after escaping to a physical sanctuary, however, would take work. As Luciano Minerbi explains, the puʻuhonua "is a corrective institution for spiritual and character growth and transformation."[23] After entering the place of refuge, lawbreakers had to be absolved by the gods. This process required ritual so that the person could be "reborn."

While Puʻuhonua o Puʻuhuluhulu was certainly not established to absolve people of their crimes, it is important to think of it as a potential place for uncomfortable "rebirthing," cleansing, and preparation. By "uncomfortable" I am not implying that rising in awareness, in activism, and in commitment to the movement must be troublesome or distressing. In fact, it can be, and is often described as, a beautiful process. Instead, I mean that sometimes in order to come back to the honua (earth), we must shed some of our out-dated ideas, our preconceived notions, and even the residual prejudices that we may be carrying from the past. This is why I've chosen to frame Kahiki as a sanctuary. The function of a puʻuhonua is not to be a permanent place of residence. People went to sanctuaries when they needed them, and the pur-pose of those places or people was to give them an avenue for reintegrating into society after threats were gone or after wrongdoings had been forgiven. Kahiki is the same. We are not meant to live in Kahiki permanently. Kahiki, after all, is a concept more than it is a concrete place. Therefore, we are meant to visit, leave, and then return to it—whether in memory, in active recall, or in song, chant, or story—whenever we need comfort, encouragement, or sometimes even harsh lessons and reminders.

Aloha ʻĀina

Before progressing, it is important that I explain one of the motivations be-hind this work, what drives the movement at Mauna Kea, and what inspires all of our protective actions for the honua. As a Kanaka Maoli who was raised in the wake of the Hawaiian Renaissance—a movement beginning in the late 1960s and early 1970s, when "a renewed sense of identity and history as to what it meant to be a Hawaiian began to emerge"—my views of the world are undoubtedly shaped by my commitment to aloha ʻāina.[24] Aloha ʻāina, a true driving force for me in daily life, is complex and therefore not easily translated into English. Loosely interpreted it means "love of the land or of one's country" and is therefore often explained as "patriotism."[25] A number of contemporary Kanaka Maoli scholars agree, however, that the term can-not simply be equated with "patriotism," for it expresses much more than a love for the land, but an unwavering commitment and an fierce, active, and constant loyalty to all that the ʻāina represents: our sources of sustenance, our health and well-being, our political freedom, our stories and histories, and, in short, our life and survival as a people and as a nation.[26] In regard to ʻāina, Kekuewa Kikiloi explains that it "sustains our identity, continuity, and well-being as a people. It embodies the tangible and intangible values of our culture that have developed and evolved over generations."[27] Moreover, aloha ʻāina is based on viewing the land as a living ancestor. Thus, our kuleana (responsibility) to protect it stems from the way Kānaka Maoli understand our familial relationship to the ʻāina as a provider and as the foundation of our experiences. Furthermore, Noelani Goodyear-Kaʻōpua states, "The concept of aloha ʻāina has been a root of Hawaiian resistance to imperial-ism for over one hundred years . . . the *aloha* part of this phrase is an active verb, not just a sentiment. As such, it is important to think of aloha ʻāina as a practice rather than as merely a feeling or a belief."[28] Thus, aloha ʻāina is a way of *being*, a way of living and consciously working to protect our place. Additionally, though, as aloha 'āina is both a verb and a noun, it is what we *are* when we choose live this way.

It should be clarified here, however, that 'āina is more than just the land. Kekuni Blaisdell, a longtime leader in the Hawaiian sovereignty movement, explains that "'āina means 'that which feeds.'"[29] No laila [therefore], 'āina is Papa, our Earth Mother, including *wai* (all waters), *kai* (all seas), Ka Moananui (Oceania), and beyond. 'Āina is also Wākea, our Sky Father, *ea* (air), *lani* (all heavens, all suns, all moons and all stars), and beyond."[30] It is all that sustains us: land, water, *and* sky. Manulani Meyer expands this interpretation even further, arguing that the inclusion of the Pacific Ocean within a Hawaiian's view of home essentially stretches the metaphor of 'āina to *all* of our sources of sustenance, whether physical, spiritual, emotional, or otherwise.[31] Thus, to speak of 'āina, or that which feeds, is to look beyond the physical ground that we dwell upon and to honor all of those sources that nurture us. To aloha 'āina, then, is to stand to protect them.

While I did not grow up using this term regularly, like many Kānaka Maoli living in the decades after the Hawaiian Renaissance (a time that will be explored in more depth in chapter 4), I understood it, at least implicitly. I was raised, for example, by parents who were constant advocates for our people and culture: my father fought to maintain our right to gather food from the land, often finding himself at the center of heated and emotional debates about access rights and environmental protection; and my mother championed for the establishment of a Hawaiian language preschool in my hometown of Waimea on the Big Island of Hawai'i, even while history had stripped that language from her own mouth and while she worked tirelessly, at the same time, to try and learn it as an adult. Their actions eventually led my father to help create an organization dedicated to protecting our lands and waters, and my mother to eventually serve as the first director of the preschool she advocated for. I grew up with these models in my household, knowing that continuing their work—in whatever way I could—was more than just a responsibility. It was, as I would eventually come to learn, about being an aloha 'āina and acting upon that inheritance.

Although the concept of aloha 'āina is distinctly Hawaiian, the deep sense of loyalty and commitment that people have for their nation cannot be divorced from conversations about nationalisms that have been experienced and enacted throughout the world. In his seminal work on the origins of nationalism, Benedict Anderson explains that although the concept of a nation, a nationality, and even of nationalism itself are quite hard to define, the political entity of the nation—an entity that is "imagined" and therefore created—promotes deep attachments that can inspire those who belong to it to make personal sacrifices, to even die for their country if they need to.[32] Nations such as the Lāhui Hawai'i, or the Hawaiian Nation, are "imagined communities." They are "*imagined* because the members of even the smallest nation will never know most of their fellow-members, meet them, or even hear of them, yet in the minds of each lives the image of their communion."[33] The idea of a nation, therefore, allows people to be connected by that sense of attachment and belonging to a single entity, regardless of whether they will ever truly meet or know one another personally. It is this idea of a shared relationship to place and a common responsibility to it that drives the kiaʻi of Mauna Kea to come together. I know I will never meet every other kiaʻi. However, in my heart, I know that we are united in purpose, and it is that unity that inspires me.

Although what I imagine the Hawaiian Nation to be today is undoubtedly much different from what my ancestors in the nineteenth century may have imagined as they dealt with American encroachment or even what my parents imagined as they were engrossed in the Hawaiian Renaissance, I do know that I pledged loyalty to *a* Hawaiian nation at an early age. Though I may not have had a name for it, I always knew that my parents' fight was for *the people*, "the people" being those like them: Kānaka Maoli trying to live in a world that continually tried to erase them, physically and culturally. They were people, as Michael Chandler describes in regard to Indigenous communities, trying to "understand themselves, and instruct their children, in a world no longer willing to make a place for them" or in a world that continued to threaten their "persistent indigeneity."[34] Despite struggle, they were people who persisted in being Indigenous, or in being Hawaiian, and who were united in their dedication to do so and to be so. As Jonathan Osorio puts it, being Kanaka Maoli, for many, "isn't just ancestry and it isn't just cultural proficiency; being Hawaiian is ultimately about not wishing to be anything else."[35] My own sense of belonging grew from such sentiments. To *be* Kanaka Maoli meant being loyal to "the people," as vague as that grouping may have been (and as vague as it continues to be), and to our continued survival. This staunch commitment to being Kanaka Maoli first and foremost, and to working toward the betterment of the nation together, is grounded in a belief in shared kinship, one rooted in the ʻāina. It is this commitment to being Kanaka that drives my work.

With that said, the goal of this book is not to be exclusionary or wholly nationalistic. Rather, it is to find the balance between a strong sense of nationalism and regionalism, the balance of complementary and enriching identities that Epeli Hauʻofa once advocated for.[36] As a student and teacher of Pacific studies, furthermore, I hope to locate this work in the vā, or the space between, using my own Hawaiian identity not as a means of distancing myself from other peoples and places but as an opportunity to connect. In her articulations of Pacific studies, Teaiwa explained that it is *not* nationalistic or ethnocentric.[37] Rather, it encourages comparative analyses as a means of understanding and acknowledging both similarities and cultural and historical specificities. It also promotes a shared obligation to the region, not a homogenizing regional identity but the knowledge that realizing our relationships to each other can "help us to act together for the advancement of our collective interests."[38] Thus, although this book centers on Kahiki, a uniquely Hawaiian concept, it does so as a means of escaping the insularity that can come with fierce nationalisms, and of finding ways to work together across oceans, islands, and nations. As mentioned previously, Kānaka Maoli are not the only people with a concept like Kahiki. The idea of an ancestral homeland does not belong to us alone. Therefore, perhaps by focusing so intently on my own, I can also provide a means for others to do the same, using their own words, languages, metaphors, stories, and ancestral migrations to explore how to use these "homelands" as spaces for growth.

My Kahiki

As a Kanaka Maoli, I can say that I wrote this book in Kahiki, in a land beyond the shores of Hawai'i. Though it was difficult to leave the lands that taught me, and the mountain that shaded me, my physical departure from Hawai'i was necessary for me to truly experience the power of Kahiki. When I started this research in Aotearoa as an eager PhD student in 2012, I realized that if I was going to study Kahiki as a place beyond Hawai'i, I needed to go there, not just intellectually, but physically and spiritually. Making that journey, I would find, would bring me closer to "home," closer to understanding my place, my role, my responsibilities, and, truly, myself. It was in Kahiki, for example, that I was able to truly connect to the idea of a homeland and to experience, firsthand, the way that my attachments to a particular place continue to feed my perspectives and to influence my voice, no matter how far away from it I may be. It gave me the chance to think about my kūpuna, the first ones to migrate from Kahiki to Hawai'i, who brought with them memories of their home, memories that would become so deeply entrenched in the Hawaiian consciousness that we continue to honor them today. This connection to homeland became even more apparent as I completed my PhD in 2015. As I worked toward finishing it, a group of Kānaka Maoli and other supporters stood on Mauna Kea. A year prior, the University of Hawai'i—an institution that I am both an alumna and a past employee of—had voted to sublease land on the summit of Mauna Kea for the construction of the TMT. As I wrote the last bits of my thesis, contemporary aloha 'āina stood upon that mountain, dedicated to protecting it and to putting an end to the further desecration of our land, our people, and our ways of life.

Living thousands of miles away, I felt useless. I was in Kahiki, in Aotearoa, yearning to plant my feet on the summit of our mauna. However, I had crossed the equator and was now an ocean away from my homeland.

In that moment of crossing, my Hawai'i became my "Kahiki." It became the place that I held in my heart, the place that life came from, the place that cultivated my attachments to 'āina and that inspired my aloha. It became the place that I would always shout for, raising my voice courageously as my ancestors did, putting my words into print as those who wrote in the Hawaiian language newspapers did, and standing steadfast, rooted, and grounded in the knowledge and guidance of those who came before me. It was my physical separation from Hawai'i that taught me something about how my kūpuna may have dealt with leaving their homelands, how they may have perhaps articulated their aloha for more than just the lands they migrated to but also for the lands from which they came, and for the ocean that connected them. It reminded me, as Pualani Kanahele argues, that "some natives have primal instincts so embedded that despite generations of exposure to the thinking mind and 'civilization,' ancestral behavior surfaces."[39] Perhaps that sense of aloha 'āina that I felt in my na'au, in my gut, or that sense of commitment to protect a homeland, even while an ocean away, was something that my kūpuna once experienced. Perhaps it was an "ancestral behavior" surfacing, or resurfacing. Being in Kahiki allowed me that.

In what now seems to be an appropriate twist in life events, I find myself back in Aotearoa, years after finishing my PhD, now living and working here, teaching Pacific studies. I am once again away from Hawai'i, once again given the opportunity to reflect on what it means to be in "Kahiki," and to even consider the problematics of calling this place by a Hawaiian name (something I had done without enough critical evaluation while completing my thesis, and therefore something that will be explored in more depth in chapter 2). Revising my previous work and completing this book, I believe, may have been able to occur only here. This is where this research started, and this is the place that provided me with the chance to look back, across the ocean, to my home, once again calling upon the power of Kahiki and learning from the reversal of positions as I consider my life in this country and what it means to feel increasingly "at home" on someone else's land. My own grappling with the complexities of being Indigenous in a place that I am not Indigenous to, a key focus of chapter 5, has led me to think of Kahiki in more generative ways. How can the acknowledgment of ancestral connections lead to more intentional understandings of specific colonial contexts and the obligations that come with them? While Kahiki *could* enable me to claim Indigeneity to the region, how might such an identity disrupt Indigenous movements in places where claiming firstness matters and has to matter? Considering these questions urges me to think of Kahiki not as a safety net for claiming belonging to the region, and making myself or others feel comfortable, but instead as a tie that makes us accountable to each other, even if and when that accountability means interrogating ourselves and our actions. Kahiki, then, can be a space for learning how to reenter the region and the world renewed, rebirthed, and reconnected.

Kahiki as Sanctuary

As explained previously, each chapter of this book will engage with Kahiki as a sanctuary. In some chapters, Kahiki will be a place of comfort, an empowering place with the ability to energize and motivate our movements. In others, Kahiki will be an uncomfortable and challenging place, exposing necessary tensions to feel and work through for the betterment of the region (and in some cases, the world). Each section, despite the change in focus and intent, will be guided by the same grounding belief stated simply and directly in the proverb: "Aia ke ola i Kahiki." There is indeed life to be found in Kahiki. Therefore, each chapter has been written with the confidence that there is something of value—whether in the form of reconstructed knowledges, critical inquiries, new interpretations, or growing understandings—to be found in examining this enduring place of intrigue and connection. It is then from this sanctuary that I will propose new/renewed ways of engaging with Kahiki, using it in contemporary times, and giving it function for now and into the future.

Chapter 1 will begin by examining the potential role Kahiki can play in our protective actions for lands, waters, and oceans around the world. In exploring connections to Kahiki, both genealogical and otherwise, I will argue that our environments, and the grave state of our planet, require us to act upon an expanded vision and connection to Kahiki that will enable us to push both our protective actions and our deep and fierce aloha ʻāina to the world. Drawing on specific examples of environmental damage, I will weave in and out of discourses of national and regional identities and responsibilities, will work at the tensions in discussions of migration and Indigeneity, and will comment on what it truly means to be "close to nature." In this chapter, while looking downward and inward at Kahiki as part of who we are as Kānaka Maoli, I will also use it to look outward, even beyond our region. Starting here, I believe is imperative so that we can prioritize conversations about the health of our planet and how Indigenous concepts such as Kahiki may help us in saving it.

Chapter 2 will examine Kahiki as a name, a name that may have once referred to a specific place but that over time became an amalgamation of places, peoples, histories, and memories, thus losing some of its specificity. After tracing the genealogy of change embedded in this one name, as recorded in historical accounts, I will then break Kahiki down into parts, seeing what its root words can reveal about its potential in encouraging a critical (re)examination of our relationships in the Pacific and in our solidarity movements. In this chapter, Kahiki will be the type of sanctuary that must be visited for deep reflection and for challenging our perceptions of ourselves and of each other. In visiting this space of difficult contemplation, I hope to examine how and why we come together at particular moments and for specific reasons. In doing so, I will unpack some of the problematics of umbrella terms used in the region, including "Indigenous," to propose how we might think differently about the role of colonization in our ongoing articulations of Pacific connection.

Chapter 3 will look at historical engagements with Kahiki, specifically in the nineteenth century as Kānaka Maoli were writing, speaking, and debating their relationships with the outside world, and in particular, with the United States. In this chapter, I will examine a specific wānana, or prophecy, that has been central in current sovereignty movements, including daily ceremonies at Puʻuhonua o Puʻuhuluhulu, but that also has a long and complicated history. Through this particular prophecy, I hope to highlight historical agency, or the ability of our kūpuna to use Kahiki in ways that suited their political agendas, whether they were for or against American imperialism. I also hope that this chapter will emphasize the fact that what Kahiki means, or has meant, reflects the people who engage with it and who shift its meaning with purpose. In this chapter, I will also consider concepts such as radical hope and radical sovereignty, and their role not just in the past but in also creating our futures.

Chapter 4 will examine engagements with Kahiki in the context of the Hawaiian Renaissance and, in particular, in the story of a single-hulled canoe named *Mauloa*. In doing so, it will comment on some of the complexities and binds of cultural revitalization and Indigenous persistence. In addition to confronting some of the problematics of recontextualization, an integral part of cultural maintenance and survival, I hope to use the story of *Mauloa* to reflect on cultural constructions both in the past and in the present. In this chapter, Kahiki will be framed as a sanctuary in which we find the freedom—without needing approval from the state or any colonial power—to continue doing and being in the now, and, further, where we can combat any challenges to our authenticity.

Chapter 5 will grapple with the complexities of recalling Kahiki when Kānaka Maoli are in "Kahiki," or when we are outside of Hawaiʻi. In an effort to contribute to understandings of Indigeneity in the Pacific, I will offer a non-Māori perspective on an issue facing the Indigenous peoples of Aotearoa. In this chapter, I will examine my own positionality as someone who recognizes ancestral connections but also as someone who refuses to find too much comfort in them, particularly in another settler colonial context. In analyzing current pressing issues in this country, I hope to unravel and expose the logics of erasure being enacted in them while also arguing for how Kahiki can be a means of understanding our obligations to each other, especially when we are no longer at home.

The final chapter of this book will examine settler colonial articulations of time and space in order to present Indigenous counterparts that may be better suited for planting and nurturing our dreams. To do so, I will examine news stories about public parks and puʻuhonua in order to propose that Kahiki, as a sanctuary and as the nonphysical space from which life comes, is the ultimate expression of Indigenous space and time, one that cannot be colonized, one that cannot be coopted. It is my hope here to renew and reinvigorate Kahiki as a space in which we can always dream good dreams, a space where there are no limits on our imaginings of the future.

1

THE EDGE

Kahiki and Protective Action

In the midst of the ongoing movement to protect Mauna Kea, I was asked to reflect on what gives ʻŌiwi, or Indigenous peoples, an "edge" in the world. This prompting came from a friend of mine who currently works at a school for Kanaka Maoli students. She wanted me to offer some thoughts about how their being Indigenous could give them an advantage. This was to combat any notions of inferiority arising from common experiences of marginalization that often come with being Hawaiian in Hawaiʻi. As may be expected, especially given the common assumptions made about Indigenous peoples, I immediately thought about our connection to ʻāina, our connection to the lands and waters that nourish us. I thought about genealogies and intimate relationships with place. I thought about aloha ʻāina, or the deep love that motivates our protective actions. I thought about all of the kiaʻi standing at Mauna Kea, all of the kaitiaki standing at Ihumātao, and wondered about what it was, exactly, that made us willing to give everything to our movements for ʻāina, for whenua, for moana (ocean), for place. While "closeness to nature" as a trope has actually been used against Indigenous peoples in insidious ways, it *is* indeed a kind of closeness and relationship that propels us. As I thought more, however, and as I sat with news of the possible increase of police and military presence and violence on Mauna Kea, I realized that it is so much more than a connection to the natural world that does (or can) give Indigenous peoples an edge.[1] Though it saddens me to admit this, one of the things that give us a slight advantage in the world is our deep, inter-generational experience of trauma and pain. It is because we have felt our stomachs churn at the sight of desecration; it is because we have felt tears run down our cheeks after being locked out of yet another sacred space; it is because we have felt our breath get caught in our chests upon hearing the sound of another bomb hitting our land, our mother; it is because we have experienced gut-wrenching anguish, in other words, that we have the edge: the advantage and the opportunity to use our grief to fight for a better world.

I've been asked on occasion to speak to students about the concept of aloha ʻāina and what motivates us to stand for place. As explained in the introduction to this book, aloha ʻāina is not easily defined in English. In fact, simple translations never capture it in all of its beauty and complexity. Aloha ʻāina is both a verb and a noun. It is the act of caring for and protect-ing ʻāina (or everything that feeds) and it is what we become when we do so. Thus, we both aloha ʻāina, or care for our lands, oceans, and waters, and *are* aloha ʻāina, or patriots and protectors of Hawaiʻi. In recent years, I've come to explain this concept as a fierce and ferocious love of place. It is the willing-ness to do anything and everything possible to protect our natural world, our ancestors, and ourselves. Though not referring to it as "aloha ʻāina," Naomi Klein describes this ferocious love as seen in other Indigenous communi-ties around the world. It is the kind of love, she explains, that "no amount of money can extinguish" because "what is being fought for is an identity, a culture, a beloved place that people are determined to protect to pass on to their grandchildren, and that their ancestors may have paid for with great sacrifice."[2] Her words remind us that although aloha ʻāina as a concept is unique to my kūpuna, the idea of loving your environment so intensely isn't. In fact, as I have argued in previous work, this kind of love not only exists elsewhere—albeit in different forms and with different names—but can be (and should be) reactivated, cultivated, and grown everywhere.[3]

In one of my talks in 2019, I spoke with a group of university students, most of them in their second or third years of study, and most of them white. Knowing that *all* people have the capacity to develop a sense of what Yi-Fu Tuan calls "topophilia," or "the affective bond between people and place or setting," I endeavored to bring that affection for place out of them, to the surface.[4] We started by thinking about places as being nourishing: physically, spiritually, emotionally, and imaginatively. We thought about the places that sustain us, the places where we feel most comfortable, most inspired, most "at home" in our own skin. We sat with the memories of those places for a minute and then wrote poetry. I asked the students to complete the following, filling in the blank and finishing the sentences:

A place that sustains me is _____.
If you were to see it, you'd see . . .
If you were to hear it, you'd hear . . .
If you were to taste it, you'd taste . . .
If you were to feel it, you'd feel . . .
If you were to be nourished by it, you'd be . . .

My goal here was to encourage the students to think differently about place, to push themselves to consider how a place might sound, taste, feel. I wanted to wake up what Robin D. G. Kelley calls their "poetic knowledge," or their ability to imagine and see beyond imposed limits on their creativity.[5] When they were finished, I asked them to share their "love of place" with a neighbor. The room erupted and overflowed with stories, with memories, with laughter, and for some, with hints of sadness and longing. When I asked for volunteers to then share their poems with the rest of the class, we watched students light up, speaking about their places with affection, sighing, smiling, telling stories about trees in backyards, pets buried in the soil, parents teaching them outside, picking fruit, and making their favorite foods. One student even described her place as tasting like her mother's chocolate pudding: delicious and smooth. In doing this poetry exercise, the students shared bits of themselves.

To demonstrate what motivates our current actions to protect ʻāina, or to protect all of our natural environments, I then asked them to imagine how they'd feel if their places were destroyed: bulldozed, trees cut down, buried loved ones unearthed, memories uprooted from the soil. We sat with the discomfort of those imaginings before I said, "That, that punch in your gut, that's what it is to aloha ʻāina, that's what it means to love fiercely, to love place *in* and *out* of pain." My aim in these exercises is never to make students feel bad, or to leave them feeling disoriented and distressed. My aim, instead, is to use that experience of pain, however brief, to galvanize them into understanding a bit of what displacement—something so many of our Indigenous children are already far too accustomed to—feels like. I use this, strategically, to encourage care, genuine care, for place and people, and I use it to advocate for empathy, something I fear we are quickly losing as a human race, too numbed by (or desensitized to) constant destruction. However, I do not only use this with non-Indigenous students. I also use it with Kānaka Maoli. With them, I use it as a means of encouraging all of us to think bigger, to use the pain that already sits in so many of our bones—both generational and from our own lifetimes—to think about lands and peoples beyond our shores, in Kahiki.

In this chapter, I will therefore reflect on the "edge" that Kānaka Maoli have and how we can use our experiences of displacement, disruption, and dispossession as a call to be better stewards of the earth. It is about using that "punch in the gut" as motivation to live better, not just for our own lands and waters but for all places. In doing so, I will examine connections to Kahiki, both genealogical and otherwise, arguing that our world, and the grave state of our planet, requires us to act upon an expanded vision and connection to Kahiki. In our contemporary times—as forests burn in the Amazon, as sacred and ancient birthing trees are being cut down in Djab Wurrung territory,[6] as islands in the Pacific continue to be threatened by rising sea levels (even while being the smallest contributors to greenhouse gas emissions), as global temperatures continue rise, as plastic pollution monopolizes our currents and waves, as climate change threatens everything we know and love, and while some world "leaders" still refuse to do anything about it—we have to act. Therefore, drawing on specific examples of environmental damage, this chapter will argue that Kahiki, as a concept, is what we need to push both our protective actions and our deep and fierce aloha 'āina to the world. In doing so, I will frame Kahiki as a sanctuary, the kind of sanctuary that our world's environments rely upon for their futures.

Closeness to Nature

Before delving further into genealogical connections to place and how Kahiki can be used to extend the reach of our aloha, it is important to first examine "closeness to nature" as a concept. It is from this kind of closeness, after all, that people launch into protective action. Many Indigenous peoples have articulated a sense of being close to, and even one with, the natural world. Sherri Mitchell, for instance, explains it as the inability to distinguish between land, waters, and ourselves because we are all inextricably interconnected.[7] Brandy Nālani McDougall expands on this notion arguing that it is because of this interconnectedness that "human beings should act according to the values of reciprocity, sustainability, and mutual care."[8] In other words, it is to acknowledge, as Pualani Kanahele once said so simply and profoundly, "I am this land, and this land is me" and then to act upon that understanding.[9] To affect land, after all, is to affect ourselves, because there is no separation. At Pu'uhonua o Pu'uhuluhulu, the sanctuary for all kia'i at the base of Mauna Kea, it is not uncommon to see T-shirts reading, "We Are Mauna Kea," or even newly silk-screened jackets and tops reading, "We Are *Still* Mauna Kea." What these two phrases remind us of is that we were, are, and will always be 'āina. We are not only connected to the natural world, we carry it in us in the same way we carry traces and traits of our parents and grandparents, becoming the extension of genealogies that run generations back and the link that will connect genealogies running generations forward.

This "closeness to nature," however, has been critiqued as it has been, at times, used to frame Indigenous peoples in damaging ways. Barry Stephenson, for instance, argues that confining "Native place as [being] 'in' or 'close to' nature has been and remains a central trope of Eurocentric culture."[10] While this intimate connection to the earth has been celebrated by some environmentalists, such as Klein,[11] as something that can save the world, it has also been used to simultaneously dehumanize and incarcerate Indigenous peoples in time and space. As Stephenson explains further, "even positive stereotypes [like an affectionate bond to place] may be implicated in the processes of colonization."[12] Colonial attitudes toward land are based on territory building, extraction, and conquest. They are not based on care or on nurturing relationships. In fact, in regard to settler colonialism, it is place (and not people) that is at the center of the colonial project.[13] Therefore, the relationship between Indigenous peoples and their places is an impediment to processes of colonialism. Any sense of "closeness" that keeps people attached to their lands, in other words, must be severed and destroyed. This results in displacement, not just the detachment of peoples from lands but also the violent disarticulation of personhood. Further, since land is viewed as a possession, as something to conqueror, tame, and take for oneself or one's country, any people who are viewed as being so close to nature as to be deemed "nature" themselves can also be conquered. This has been, and continues to be, the experience of many around the world.

Further complicating the "close to nature" trope is that it can also become something used to measure Indigeneity, even by Indigenous peoples. If one must experience oneself as being connected to the 'āina, for example, in order to be Kanaka, then what about all of those who are disconnected? Does this then, as Jeffrey Sissons suggests, result in a kind of "eco-indigenism" that "primitivizes indigenous peoples living in settler states who have adopted urban lifestyles," or that, in other instances, challenges their "authenticity"?[14] This closeness to nature can also result in what others have called "eco-incarceration," or the binding of people to place while also restricting their movement (implying that movement away from place will make someone less connected and therefore less Indigenous).[15] These conceptualizations of intimate proximity to nature lock Indigenous peoples to place while also locking them to colonial temporalities: always stuck in the past, unable to move out and to move forward. Considering the problematics of the "closeness to nature" trope, it then becomes essential to use Indigenous knowledges to articulate our own understandings of place and connection. In Aotearoa, Lynette Carter says that the idea that one can only be home (close to land) *or* away (thereby disconnected) is, quite simply, "not relevant to Māori life."[16] As she argues, "Peoples are not locked into specific places, rather . . . the place is an anchor for origins, culture, and identity" no matter where you are.[17] Thus, a sense of oneness and interconnectedness to nature is not predicated on being in one place permanently and indefinitely. Rather, it is about seeing ourselves as connected anywhere and everywhere, cultivating aloha 'āina wherever we are. Kahiki, I believe, is our opportunity to do so, at once combating restrictive notions of Indigeneity imposed on us while also pushing us out into the region and the world through protective action.

We Are 'Āina, We Are Kahiki

Before progressing, I must acknowledge the fact that not all Indigenous peoples (and certainly not all Kānaka Maoli) see themselves as being "one with nature." Therefore, my intent here is not to standardize Indigeneity or to propose one "authentic" Indigenous experience. To do so would be both fruitless and impossible. Other Pacific scholars before me, such as Albert Wendt and Epeli Hau'ofa, have argued against static notions of culture and the impossibilities of homogeneity.[18] Therefore, my aim here in foregrounding a connection to place is to pull on the experiences of those who *do* choose to act upon a genealogical relationship with 'āina. As touched upon in my poetry exercise previously, I think bonds between place and people—whether they are seen as genealogical or not—can be nurtured and grown in everyone. This is *not* at all to say that everyone can claim Indigeneity based on affection (as this would severely interfere with the work of Indigenous peoples, particularly in settler colonies). This *is* to say that all people can learn to treat place respectfully because of that affection, and even more importantly, can also learn to respect the rights of the Indigenous peoples wherever they live. All of this is to say that "closeness to nature" is not something to lock us to place and time. It is not something to incarcerate us while simultaneously providing opportunity for the Indigenization of non-Indigenous peoples. Instead, "closeness to nature" is something to share, grow, and use productively for the planet. That, for Kānaka Maoli who already experience themselves/ourselves as being connected, is our "edge," and far more importantly, our contribution.

For many Kānaka, our relationship with 'āina, and our inability to be detached from land and water, comes from seeing ourselves as being related. It comes from knowing and articulating mo'okū'auhau. Often understood quite broadly as "genealogy," mo'okū'auhau may be better described as "a carefully and critically guarded historical science," a science that links us to more than just our blood relatives but also to the environment, to plants and animals, and to the wider universe.[19] Breaking the word down into parts, David A. Chang explains that "kū'auhau" is genealogy, whereas "mo'okū'auhau" "suggests the narration of the ancestry."[20] "It is the mo'o [or succession]," he explains further, "that takes kū'auhau (ancestry) and turns it into mo'okū'auhau (a tracing of a lineage in a series, a genealogical narrative)."[21] What this implies is that mo'okū'auhau is not just something we have or are born into but something we work at and *do* mindfully and strategically. Genealogies, for instance, were often meticulously memorized and enacted for political reasons, particularly by chiefs justifying their status as rulers, and later by contemporary Hawaiians justifying their claims to land, place, and Indigenous rights.[22]

It is this latter use of moʻokūʻauhau that becomes central in movements to protect ʻāina. It is, for example, what motivates actions on Mauna Kea. In citing a genealogical chant called "He Kanaenae no ka Hanau ana o Kauikeaouli," which is a birth chant for Kauikeaouli (Kamehameha III), Leon Noʻeau Peralto explains that it tells of a direct relationship between Kānaka Maoli and the mauna, known in the chant as "Mauna a Wākea," or the "Mauna (Child) of Wākea": "Born of the union between Papahānaumoku and Wākea [two of our oldest ancestors], Mauna a Wākea is an elder sibling of Hāloa, the aliʻi [the chief and our human ancestor]. As such, both the Mauna and Kanaka are instilled, at birth, with particular kuleana [responsibilities] to each other."[23] In this chant, Papahānaumoku ("Papa who Births Islands," considered our Earth Mother) and Wākea (our Sky Father) are the common ancestors to all Hawaiians *and* the creators of the land upon which we live. It is through this understanding that statements such as "We are Mauna Kea" or "We are ʻĀina" make sense. In coming from the same source, the same ancestors, we not only justify our rights *in* and *to* place but sustain our enduring stewardship of ʻāina as well.

In acknowledging these intimate relationships to place, any genealogical claim of connection to lands and waters beyond Hawaiʻi can be seen as potentially troublesome or contradictory. Kahiki, for example, is our ancestral memory of migration. It is the knowledge that our kūpuna came from other places in Oceania before arriving in Hawaiʻi, establishing themselves as the first peoples in the islands. Therefore, assertions such as "We are Kahiki," something I've come to embrace in both the writing of my PhD thesis and now the writing of this book, can be read as conflicting with notions of "We are ʻĀina." In Aotearoa, Alice Te Punga Somerville explores this predicament, asking, "How do Māori articulate and negotiate the rather difficult intersection between discourses of migration (we came from Hawaiki on waka [canoes]) and claims to indigeneity (we've always been here)?"[24] In reaching back selectively (as strands of moʻokūʻauhau can be either foregrounded or sidelined intentionally), I believe it is possible to work in this difficult intersection, revealing that these two seemingly contradictory identities need not be in tension.

One prominent moʻokūʻauhau demonstrating the ability to be both grounded in place and transitory comes from the story of a great voyaging chief named Moʻikeha. My focus on "roots and routes,"[25] as the popular phrase goes, is not meant to imply that these are the only identities available to choose from. It is, instead, to work through the often-confronting tensions existent between them. I was first introduced to Moʻikeha and his adventures in the 1990s after the canoe renaissance that began in Hawai'i in the 1970s and that led to a revival in noninstrument navigation and wayfinding in Polynesia (topics that will be explored further in chapter 4). As a young girl at the time, I was taught to dance and chant of his travels as further proof that Kānaka Maoli come from a long history of courageous and skilled ancestors, without whom we would not exist. Thus, the way his story was re-presented to me reflected the cultural and political environment of the time: a couple of decades after the start of the Hawaiian Renaissance and the equally important (and complimentary) Hawaiian movement, sometimes called the Hawaiian sovereignty movement, which "began as a battle for land rights but would evolve, by 1980, into a larger struggle for native Hawaiian autonomy."[26] Therefore, retelling and even celebrating stories such as that of Mo'ikeha had power: the power to restore dignity, especially after decades of Western scholars doubting the seafaring abilities of our ancestors, and some, such as Andrew Sharp, even proposing theories of accidental drift.[27] It was a means of healing from the effects of what Ngũgĩ wa Thiong'o refers to as the "cultural bomb," which sought (and still seeks) to annihilate everything from our language, customs, and names to our physical and spiritual environments and, perhaps most devastatingly, to our unity as people and our faith in our shared and individual capacities.[28] Thus, what was emphasized in Mo'ikeha's story as it was reiterated to me was contextually shaped, and is therefore reflective of the intentional use of mo'okū'auhau.

Today, in the context of our current movements to protect our sacred places, and to protect our environments at large, Mo'ikeha's story can once again be chosen and interpreted strategically to speak to these times and to our agendas and hopes *now*. More specifically, an often-recited genealogical chant contained in his story can be used to work at the intersection of grounded (national) and routed (regional or even global) identities. In the section below I will engage in the labor of examining this chant closely in an effort to demonstrate how we are both 'āina and Kahiki, and how, drawing inspiration from Lynette Carter, seeing these identities in tension is simply not relevant to Kānaka Maoli lives.[29]

Papa Travels, Papa Creates

According to Joseph Poepoe's serial column in the Hawaiian-language newspaper *Ka Na'i Aupuni*, after one voyage to Hawai'i from Tahiti, Mo'ikeha's navigator, a man named Kamahualele, stood aboard their canoe and chanted:

> Eia Hawaii, he moku, he kanaka,[30]
> He kanaka Hawaii—e
> He kanaka Hawaii;
> He kama na Kahiki[31]

He pua alii mai Kapaahu,
Mai Moaulanuiakea Kanaloa,
He mokupuni[32] na Kahiko, laua o Kapulanakehau,
Na Papa i hanau.[33]
[Behold Hawaiʻi, an island, a human,
Hawaiʻi is a human
Hawaiʻi is indeed a human;
A child of Kahiki
A chiefly child from Kapaahu,
From Moaulanuiakea Kanaloa,
An island of Kahiko and Kapulanakehau
It was Papa who gave birth].[34]

In his chant, Kamahualele recited a genealogy linking Hawaiʻi and Kahiki in a parent-child relationship, thereby suggesting that there would be no Hawaiʻi if Kahiki did not exist. Conceptually, though, as I will discuss later in this chapter, since Kahiki as an idea is unique to Hawaiʻi, we could perhaps also argue that Kahiki would not survive without Hawaiʻi, thus meaning they have more of a coconstitutive relationship.

After mentioning Kahiki, the chant lists other place names, including Kapaʻahu and Moaʻulanuiākea Kanaloa. The precise location of these two places is uncertain, though some accounts do place them in or around Tahiti.[35] In researching the names of various distant lands beyond Hawaiʻi, David A. Chang cites Kahiki as the most prominent.[36] This could perhaps be due to its dual function. In this case, for example, we see Kahiki operating as a specific place (in this instance, Tahiti) and *not* just the general idea of an ancestral homeland outside of Hawaiʻi. When listed with other names, such as Kapaʻahu and Moaʻulanuiākea, we are able to see that Kahiki was just one of many names for places outside of Hawaiʻi. Kahiki, however, as noted in the introduction to this book, was not only the most referenced and well known but was also the one that took on new meanings over time, perhaps even replacing other names we may not even know existed.

Although we are not sure of the exact location of all of these places, and although stories of them often contain what may be considered fantastical elements (such as a woman birthing land, as in the chant above), we cannot dismiss them as being mere myths. Chang argues for the validity and the importance of these places, stating, "The fact that they are not on maps, that gods dwelled there, and that wondrous things happened there does not mean, however, that they were 'mythical,' 'mystical,' or 'mythological' lands, as Americans treated them throughout the twentieth century. In Hawaiian global geography, the presence of gods and other-than-human beings in far-off lands does not make a space different from home. It makes it like home."[37] Chang's words are reminiscent of the coconstitutive relationship mentioned earlier. Though Hawai'i may be the child, younger and having come forth from lands and peoples beyond, Kahiki also survives because of Hawai'i and because of its prominence in our genealogies and narratives of migration. Hawai'i, a place of gods, a place where wondrous things did happen (and continue to happen), is a reflection of Kahiki and is assurance that the memory of our connection to ancestral places will live on both *in* us and *through* our actions.

After listing specific place names, Kamahualele's chant then acknowledges three important figures in Hawaiian mo'okū'auhau.[38] Kahiko and Kapulanakēhau are the parents of Wākea. Wākea, as mentioned earlier, is considered to be one of the oldest ancestors of Kānaka Maoli because it was from his union with Papahānaumoku (often referred to as Papa) that our lands were created. In the chant cited above, Papa is the one who gives birth to the child Hawai'i. There are many chants and stories referencing Papa and Wākea and the subsequent "birthing" of the Hawaiian Islands. However, interpretations of these narratives vary. In his analysis of them, for example, Poepoe states,

> I ka moolelo o ka Papa hanau ana mai i keia pae moku . . . ua
> kuhihewa kekahi poe, o ia mau hoike ana mai a na mele, no ko
> Papa hanau maoli ana mai ia i keia mau pae moku, oiai nae o ka
> mea pololei maoli he mau kuauhau ia e hoike ana i ko Papa hanau
> ana i kana mau keiki.[39]

> [In the story regarding Papa's birthing of this archipelago . . .
> some people have misinterpreted what is shown in these chants to
> be Papa's actual delivery of the islands. However, in truth, these
> are genealogies revealing the birth of Papa's (human) children.]

Whether birthing the islands themselves or traveling to Hawai'i and giving birth to the first Kānaka to be born, Papa is regarded as our collective mother and our common ancestor. Despite Poepoe's analysis, many of us today continue to revere her as the very land upon which we live. "Papahānaumoku," as Brandy Nālani McDougall explains, "embodies the 'āina even as she is able to create more 'āina."[40] Thus, she is our mother and is the land we stand to protect, the land that we aloha deeply and fiercely with everything we have.

In honoring Papa, though, it is important to remember that she was from Kahiki.[41] Therefore, although her story is often used in conversations of rootedness—claiming that Hawaiians have always been in Hawai'i, that the islands were created first and Kānaka Maoli birthed second—the truth is that our genealogies come from Papa's initial movement from Kahiki,[42] a land outside of Hawai'i, to our place in the Pacific, where she either created new land, the people to populate it, or both. Thus, while we may want to highlight certain portions of our genealogies over others, often to coincide with our political agendas that depend upon narratives of roots and Indigeneity, we cannot deny the fact that Kahiki is, and will always be, part of our moʻokūʻauhau. Papa herself is proof that we are both Hawaiʻi and Kahiki simultaneously, and her stories provide us with the opportunity to reflect on how these identities need not exist in constant tension but, like Hawaiʻi and Kahiki themselves, can be coconstitutive parts of what makes us whole.

The Edge

The work of moʻokūʻauhau, or of learning our "historical science" of connection, gives us the chance to also use genealogies in new (or perhaps renewed) ways. As explained at the start of this chapter, I believe it is the understanding, and the generational and personal experience of displacement, that can be used to both build and sustain empathy and to inspire protective actions for our environments. Kahiki, as a genealogical concept, is critical in this process. As Kānaka, Kahiki proves that we are both the land we live on and a link to the Pacific spaces from which our kūpuna came. Importantly, however, and as noted elsewhere in this book, once Hawaiians began to interact with peoples from outside of Hawaiʻi and Oceania, Kahiki also became a general term to refer to *all* lands beyond our shores. Thus, I believe we can use this awareness of all places to expand our sense of attachment to ʻāina, putting ourselves in the position to understand the pain and struggle being experienced around the world at the destruction of our environments. In other words, while we cannot (and should not want to) claim a sense of belonging to all lands and waters, what our experiences of the pain of aloha ʻāina can do is help us to recognize and act upon the need to protect all places *as if* they were our own, or as if they were part of us, unable to be distinguished, unable to be detached, because even if we cannot trace genealogies to them, someone else can (and most likely, already does). In doing so, I believe we can also reclaim "closeness to nature" as an Indigenous descriptor and as an Indigenous reality, proving that we can be stewards acting upon our collective responsibility to the life of our planet from whenever we are.

When my friend asked me to think about what gives our Hawaiian students an edge in the world, I knew that if I could draw upon their understanding of aloha ʻāina that I could then, perhaps, use Kahiki to make them think about lands and peoples they may have never seen (or will never see) in their lifetimes. In Hawaiʻi, where many of us are engaged in fights for place and work tirelessly to protect our immediate environments, thinking about or even caring about other places may seem like a luxury, something you do only if and when you have the time to so, or something you do because all of the places around you are safe from harm. Caring about everything "beyond," however, is essential if we are going to truly care about the lands beneath our feet and the oceans surrounding them. One place that exemplifies this, and that have I have written about previously, is Kamilo Beach on the Big Island of Hawai'i.[43] I've used this beach as an example in various talks, citing it as a place that has never been, and will never be, cut off from the rest of the world.

Kamilo lies in the path of the North Pacific Gyre, a huge system of rotating currents that once brought treasures to the shoreline. Today, however, given the disgustingly large amount of plastic trash circulating in our planet's oceans, Kamilo has fallen victim to this indestructible substance of convenience and disposability, with an estimated 90 percent of the waste found on the beach being plastic.[44] As most of the trash on Kamilo comes from the currents the beach is named for (the word "milo" means "to curl, twist, or whirl as water"), each individual piece of garbage serves as a symbol of interconnectedness. Though a small portion of the trash undoubtedly comes from residents of Hawai'i, most of it does not come from people living on the island. Instead, it comes from afar, from other countries and from other people who may not even know Kamilo exists. Therefore, as I explain to students, it is through trash (unfortunately) that we can see—in very tangible and destructive ways—how our actions in one place can (and will) affect the lives of others elsewhere. The heartbreak I feel in looking at Kamilo being swallowed in a sea of trash because of plastic debris coming from other places and peoples beyond Hawai'i is the same pain and anguish someone else may feel at the sight of their own places being polluted by what *I* contribute to the world. We are all interconnected. Kahiki reminds us of this. Therefore, I believe it is imperative that we use Kahiki not just to remember connections but to also hold ourselves accountable to them.

Another glaring example of interconnectedness has to do with climate change. In a 2018 government report from the Republic of the Marshall Islands, it was recorded that the Marshalls, "one of the world's lowest-lying and climate vulnerable countries . . . may only contribute 0.00001% of global greenhouse gas emissions."[45] Thus, islanders there, along with others in places such as Tuvalu and Kiribati, are having to suffer the consequences of rising sea levels at a disproportionately higher rate than those in countries with the most greenhouse gas emissions. Like the trash washing up on Kamilo Beach, this is evidence of the fact that our actions and our lives in individual places, no matter where we happen to be, will affect others. Thus we have to escape the assumption that care comes with proximity, or that distance detaches us from responsibility, and we must embrace the fact that the future of our planet depends on us changing the ways we live. Kahiki, as the knowledge of our connection to places beyond Hawai'i, is the tool to motivate Kānaka to think differently about their/our place in the world.

This current example is especially pertinent in Hawai'i because of the Compact of Free Association that enables islanders from the Federated States of Micronesia, the Republic of the Marshall Islands, and the Republic of Palau the right to migrate to the United States as "nonimmigrants" "without durational limit," many of them opting to migrate to Hawai'i.[46] What might seem as charity on the part of the United States is actually a partial attempt at compensation for the destruction of islands in Micronesia by America. In regard to the Marshalls, from 1946 to 1958, the United States detonated sixty-seven nuclear bombs there. According to Julian Aguon, "If you take the output of the radioactive energy yield of these 67 bombs, it is the rough equivalent of 1.7 Hiroshima shots every day for 12 years."[47] In his book *What We Bury at Night: Disposable Humanity*, Aguon includes the memories of islanders who suffered, and who continue to suffer, the ongoing effects of the bombings. In their accounts, they tell heartbreaking stories of their hair falling out, their skin peeling off, women giving birth to "grape babies," and islanders suffering and dying from many different kinds of cancer.[48] The treatment of the people in those islands was inhumane, to say the least. It is now in part because of the atrocities that they've suffered that many migrate to Hawai'i in search of better medical and social care.

Unfortunately, not all residents in Hawai'i understand this. Therefore, rather than being a welcoming place of understanding, Hawai'i has become a hotbed for racial tension. In an online article, Anita Hofschneider exposes the ongoing racism against Micronesians in Hawai'i, stating that residents "don't understand why they're here" and therefore retaliate against them, calling them derogatory names such as "cockroaches" and "calling on people to 'hunt' them."[49] Though Hofschneider had hoped that the situation would have gotten better in Hawai'i since her first arrival to the islands in 2011, she reported, quite sadly, that in 2018 it hadn't. The problem is exacerbated by the fact that many who come to Hawai'i equate the island with America. This is glaringly obvious in the book *People and Cultures of Hawai'i*, in which the editors, John F. McDermott and Naleen Naupaka Andrade, not only take Hawai'i's status as the fiftieth state as a given (despite the wealth of scholarship proving the illegality of the state and challenging this outdated, historical assumption), but also frame Hawai'i as the "Hawaiian Stewpot" "with various ingredients [people] mixing together to create a common stock" in which "there was no majority group" and "everyone was part of a minority."[50] While I find their work highly problematic and damaging to Hawaiian national movements—particularly as it reinforces the place of the settler government and the subsequent relegation of Kānaka Maoli to the status of just another minority rather than the Indigenous people, topics to be explored in chapter 5—the point to be made here is that a common assumption among migrants is that they are coming to "America" and not to Hawai'i. Thus, there is misunderstanding on both sides, leading to an increase in racial animosities. All of this is to say that it can be difficult in Hawai'i to encourage Kānaka to care for a place beyond their own islands, such as places in Micronesia, especially when some of them have adopted a horribly racist attitude toward the islanders who come from them, often seeing them as people coming in, taking up space, and stealing jobs in a place where life is already difficult for so many.[51] What I have done in the past, therefore, in order to attempt—even in the smallest ways—to nurture both understanding and the hope for protective action is what I did at the beginning of this chapter: provide time and space for recognizing the weight and pain of loving place.

When I used to teach Pacific Islands studies courses at the University of Hawaiʻi–West Oʻahu, my students and I would spend a portion of the semester examining some of the most pressing, contemporary issues in the Pacific. Among them, of course, was the climate change crisis. When talking about those islands most vulnerable to the effects of climate change, I would alert students to the fact that some of the Micronesians they admitted to teasing and telling jokes about came from those places. Folded into our conversations would therefore be discussions about migration and diaspora. When we explored the reasons for migration, I'd then seek opportunities to draw links and to establish grounds for building empathy. The most obvious link—which is quite unfortunate, given the reality of having to suffer through it—is nuclear testing. Though many students in Hawaiʻi today may not know the complete history or the direct impact of bombing, they may at least know that at one time one of our islands, Kahoʻolawe, was used as a bombing target by the US military. After the infamous bombing of Pearl Harbor in 1941, the United States took Kahoʻolawe to be used for military training and firing. As a prominent activist in the fight to end the bombing of Kahoʻolawe, Walter Ritte recounts the anguish of knowing lands were being destroyed: "Pain. We really felt the pain. We really felt that the island was bleeding into the ocean."[52] Though most of my students would not have been around while the bombing was occurring, or even when it ended in 1993, they often know about it, and even more, still carry the intergenerational trauma of one's land—and extension of self—being used in such heinous ways. Thus, when we talk about that "punch in the gut" feeling that comes with the destruction of ʻāina, I reveal the gravity of the problem in places like the Marshall Islands. In doing so, I hope to provide space for a recognition of pain and an opportunity for my students to use that as their "edge," even if/when they don't yet know how to act upon it.

Kahiki as Sanctuary

While I cannot always know if this recognition will lead to protective action, I always hope that it will at the very least cultivate an expanded understanding of aloha ʻāina. Once Kānaka Maoli students are able to see, for instance, that other islanders in the Pacific have faced (and continue to face) atrocities at the hands of colonial powers, they can at least open more room in their hearts to care, discarding the layers of resentment and unfair prejudice built up over the years that have kept them from feeling connected to people and places to which they are genealogically related. How we can help, I usually suggest, is by being better human beings in the places that we are in, knowing that our actions *will* and *do* affect others. We do not have to go to the Marshalls, in other words, to help them. In fact, our actions would be far more effective if we could help to decrease global emissions by working in the spaces we currently occupy rather than traveling. Colonial powers work hard to promote a "myth of separation" in order to detach Indigenous peoples from their lands *and* from others around the world.[53] This is to isolate and disempower. In Hawaiʻi, however, our kūpuna provided us with a tool, a concept, to combat these notions of isolation and distance. Kahiki is the proof that we are always connected to lands outside of Hawaiʻi. Therefore, a new function of Kahiki can be one that uses that connection to propel collective and protective action for our worlds, action that comes from knowing the feeling, the pain, the tear-inducing, gut wrenching grief of ʻāina being destroyed. I know that no matter where I live and no matter where I teach that I will always be able to draw on the knowledge of our interrelatedness to not only push my own efforts to live in a way that helps to sustain ecological balance but that also helps others to discover their own ways to do so as well. This is Kahiki operating as a sanctuary, as the space we must go to so that we can be reminded of lands and peoples beyond our shores, and so that we can hold ourselves accountable to them, to their longevity, to their life, and to the health of our shared futures.

2

INDIGENOUS CROSSINGS

Kahiki and Solidarity

In July of 2019, a few weeks after returning to Aotearoa, following my visit to Puʻuhonua o Puʻuhuluhulu, where I had gathered with other kiaʻi dedicated to protecting Mauna Kea from destruction and desecration (as mentioned in the introduction), my students and I had a discussion about West Papua and the ongoing "slow-motion genocide" occurring there.[1] The military occupation of West Papua by Indonesia since 1963 has resulted in the torture, rape, and murder of thousands of Indigenous West Papuans. At Victoria University of Wellington, in our Pacific studies class, PASI 301: Framing the Pacific, Theorising Culture and Society, we examine the work of Pacific artists and activists who are participating in, challenging, and/or resisting dominant framings of the region's islands and peoples. In the latter half of the trimester, we use a few weeks to study specific issues that artists and activists are engaged in. One of them is the brutal and ongoing genocide in West Papua.

Between my first time teaching this course in 2015 and teaching it again in 2019, I realized that students had grown not only in their awareness of the region but also in their willingness to act upon that awareness as well.

Therefore, wanting to push our critical reflection a bit further, I decided to focus one of our class lectures on the topic of embodied activism. In doing so, we considered the question, What does it mean to be an intellectual? Using Edward Said's interpretation of intellectuals, we discussed what being "someone who visibly represents a standpoint, and someone who makes articulate representations to his or her public despite all sorts of barriers" could involve.[2] In the case of West Papua, we asked ourselves what it means, and further, what it looks like and feels like, "to represent those people and issues that are routinely forgotten or swept under the rug" (which has been the case for West Papua).[3] In our initial discussions, we thought critically about our actions and the potential pitfalls of well-intentioned "armchair activism," sometimes known as "clicktivism" or "slacktivism." This type of activism centers online activities that can be characterized as "instances of lackluster support hidden under the guise of simple 'shares,' 'likes,' and 'favorites.'"[4] In an article about slacktivism, Henrik Christensen takes an unapologetic approach in describing armchair activists, calling their activity "a pointless showcasing that does more to make the activists feel good about themselves than to address urgent political matters."[5] Conversations about slacktivism are critical in Pacific studies, especially when so many of the issues we care about are located in places we cannot access physically. We cannot go to West Papua; I cannot take my students there, nor would I want to risk doing so. Therefore, what kind of activism can we engage in that will move us beyond self-aggrandizing online posting so that we can participate in what Tagi Qolouvaki calls "mana-full resistance" that is "decolonial, contagious and muscled?"[6] Her urging, I believe, is for us to draw on the mana, or the power and influence of our ancestors, to examine the impacts of colonialism, to promote doing so throughout the region in ways that challenge hegemonic structures, and to be willing to do the work—and the metaphorical "heavy lifting"—required in the process.

This is where our discussions about embodied activism enter. As a teacher, I want to encourage my students to tap into the intelligence of their bodies so that they can carry issues—not to bear the weight of them alone—but to offer more than just platitudes and expressions of sympathy for atrocities being survived in other parts of the region. In other words, I want them to rethink Said's encouragement to "visibly represent a standpoint" and to consider what that might look like or feel like for them as individuals. We talk about self-actualization, or knowing your own skills and talents, and how powerful this can be in the process of becoming contemporary warriors.[7] This is especially important when the gravity of issues in the Pacific, combined with their physical distance, can leave students feeling helpless.[8] Further, we think about the intellectual labor that is required in being activists who do more than stand *against* something but who also know, and feel, what we are standing *for*.

With all of this being considered, one of my students took our analyses and self-reflections further by posing an important question about slacktivism in statements of solidarity. In reflecting on the recent Indigenous movements at Mauna Kea and Ihumātao, he asked about whether or not expressions of solidarity can actually detract from individual movements and blur their specific contexts and circumstances. In other words, with social media and hashtags has it become too easy—and perhaps even normalized—to conflate issues? While wanting to stand for *all* do we risk ceasing to stand confidently, purposefully, or meaningfully for one? His worry was that attempts to articulate Indigenous solidarity can be dangerous when issues or movements are grouped together in ways that do not allow for enough definition or explanation to have real impact. In our class session, a group of his classmates did a presentation featuring a slide that read: #ProtectMaunaKea, #ProtectIhumātao, #ProtectWestAustralia, #ProtectWestPapua. Without specific context, he worried that one or more of these issues could be overshadowed by another and that the severity of them as individual struggles could be neglected. His point was exacerbated by the fact that all of the hashtags, with the exception of the one for West Australia, were specific enough for people to recognize the issues being addressed. The struggle being evoked with that hashtag for West Australia, however, was too vague. When probed about it, one of the student presenters replied that it was "for the trees" but did not provide any additional information. Her statement was in reference to Djab Wurrung territory and the efforts of the Indigenous people there to save three thousand trees—some of them sacred birthing trees, and some of them eight hundred years old—from destruction. Without context, however, well-intentioned conflation led to Djab Wurrung being ignored even while being "present."

After class, my student's inquiries made me pause to consider my own activism and my willingness to group issues together in order to give activists from one movement the opportunity to know about others. In thinking about my own online activity, I had to acknowledge that he had a point, a strong and critical one. Reflecting on his in-class promptings and his courage to pose a question that would not be popular in the current age of hashtag solidarity, I was therefore motivated to reframe this chapter to consider how Kahiki—the centralizing concept of this book—could potentially promote a kind of "slackness" when thinking about and attempting to know the region. In other words, if we are not aware of the traps of conflation and homogenization that it can encourage, Kahiki could lead to more lackluster, slacktivist action. In a book framing Kahiki as a sanctuary—both in the sense that it is a place to find comfort, encouragement, and strength, as well as a place necessary for rehabilitation and sometimes difficult analysis and reflection—it is crucial that I address the potential drawbacks of using this term before suggesting how we may reclaim it in ways that are not only empowering but also responsible.

In this chapter, I will therefore examine Kahiki as a name, a name that may have once referred to a specific place but that over time became an amalgamation of places, peoples, histories, and memories, thus losing some of its specificity. After tracing the genealogy of change embedded in this one name, as recorded in historical accounts, I will then break Kahiki down into parts, seeing what its root words can reveal about its potential in encouraging a critical (re)examination of our relationships in the Pacific. This will give Kahiki new/renewed function for and in our contemporary movements. In this chapter, Kahiki will be the type of sanctuary that must be visited for deep reflection and for challenging our perceptions of ourselves and of each other. In visiting this space of difficult contemplation, I hope to examine how and why we come together at particular moments and for specific reasons. In doing so, I will unpack some of the problematics of umbrella terms used in the region, including "Indigenous," to propose how we might think differently about the role of colonization in our ongoing articulations of Pacific connection. Doing so, I believe, is essential if we are to strengthen our relationships moving forward, combating our sometimes-unconscious homogenization and providing more space to honor cultural distinctiveness. In response to my student's charge that we think critically about our actions and statements of solidarity, I hope this chapter can offer ways to engage with each other that are not "slack" but that are truly mana-full, decolonial, contagious, and muscled.

Kahiki, a Genealogy of Change

As was explored in the introduction to this book, the meanings and applications of Kahiki have been adjusted over time to accommodate changes in society. This is what has made it simultaneously fascinating and, for some seeking to define it or locate it, a bit frustrating. Examining the history of this name is essential for understanding what a single name can hold, and further, what its use today can symbolize. In the section below, therefore, I trace the genealogy of this word and its growth and change over time. Kahiki, like any evolving entity, is a combination of things. Thus, as a name, it is "a vehicle for transmitting knowledge across generations."[9] As my students and I discuss in class, however, accessing this knowledge takes time and work. The various meanings of a name like Kahiki, for instance, are not always readily available or easily accessible, especially if and when people have been cut off from the resources required to recognize or understand them.[10] We must therefore engage in the work necessary to access the complex and often tangled strands of genealogies attached to our names so that we can know how they were used and how they should (or should not) be carried into the future.

Kahiki is but one example of a single term with a complex history. What was once the name for an ancestral homeland, for instance, eventually became a term used to refer to all lands and peoples beyond Hawai'i's shores. While it is sometimes still held that Kahiki is Tahiti—given the proposition that the name originally referred to Tahiti exclusively, and the fact that "Kahiki" is the Hawaiian pronunciation of "Tahiti"—there is also ample evidence to support its use as a more general term for the Pacific region.[11] Noted nineteenth-century Hawaiian scholar Samuel Kamakau, for instance, explains that Kahiki could be used to refer to places other than Tahiti: "Ua kapa aku ka poe kahiko o Hawaii nei i na aina Borabora, a me na aina haole, o Kahiki ka inoa [The ancient people of Hawai'i called the lands of Borabora and other foreign lands Kahiki]."[12] Borabora is an island located northwest of Tahiti. Kamakau's use of "na aina," or "the lands of Borabora," then indicates that he may have been speaking about the group of islands that make up what is commonly known today as Tahiti. Using "Kahiki" for more than a single island, Kamakau shows us that its application could be broadened. Even if initially it applied only to the area of what is today referred to as French Polynesia, Kamakau proves that it could be used for "na aina haole," or for other foreign lands, as well.

Not only was Kahiki the name for places outside of Hawai'i, but, quite importantly, it was the place (or the places) that the ancestors of Hawaiians initially came from. In an account by G. W. Nakaa, the author states, "He lehulehu wale ka poe i holo mai i anei mai Kahiki mai a hoolaha kanaka [Incredibly numerous were the people who traveled here from Kahiki and spread, increasing the population]."[13] Migratory tales maintained in both oral traditions and written texts confirm this. Nineteenth- and early twentieth-century Hawaiian-language newspapers, for example, are littered with stories about great voyages from Kahiki to Hawai'i and back again, suggesting that travel did not end after the initial settlement of the islands. Although scholarship by Ben Finney suggests that Kahiki is not an ancestral homeland for Kānaka Maoli but rather a place that brave chiefs and adventurous sailors left when they traveled to an already-settled Hawai'i, some older accounts contradict this.[14] Nakaa, for example, recounts the story of a man named Hawai'iloa:

> Kaulana loa o ia i ka holo moana ana, a no Kahiki mai o ia, a
> ma kana huakai e holo ana i ka hikina, ua pae mai o ia ma anei;
> ua olelo ia, aole kanaka ma anei [i] ia wa. Ua holo aku o ia a ua
> hoi hou mai i anei me kana wahine, a hoolaha kanaka ihola
> ma anei.[15]

[He was famed as a sailor, and was from Kahiki, and on one of his voyages heading east, he landed here. It was said that there were no people here at that time. He therefore left and later returned with his wife, eventually populating this place.]

Further complicating "Kahiki" as a concept—some believing it to be an actual location, like Tahiti; others viewing it as a fantastical place from which came gods and heroes; and others using it as a general term for all lands in the Pacific—is the fact that it continued to change as people sought to understand their shifting circumstances and to make sense of their experiences in them.

Although "Kahiki" once had a Pacific base, in the nineteenth century it became a term used to refer to *all* lands outside of Hawai'i, including places such as America, Europe, and Asia, suggesting that when Hawaiians encountered foreigners from beyond the Pacific, they used existing language and concepts to make sense of them. Consequently, as interactions with foreigners increased and as Kānaka Maoli began to witness the effects of these interactions on their ways of life, Kahiki could be found at the center of discussions and debates about nationalism, identity, and nineteenth-century threats to Hawaiian sovereignty, topics that will be explored in the next chapter. An article printed in the Hawaiian-language newspaper *Ka Nupepa Kuokoa*, for example, demonstrates how Hawaiians reinterpreted statements regarding Kahiki based on their new political situations. This article reexamines a series of prophecies, some of which were made before the first Western explorers ever arrived in the islands. In reference to a wānana, or a famous prophecy, by a man named Kala'ikuahulu, it states,

O Kalaikuahulu no kai olelo aku . . . "E make ana au, i noho aku auanei oukou a i hoea mai he waa kahuna mai ke kai mai, o Kahikimakalike ka inoa, hopu iho oukou a paa, o ke kahuna ia, aole e eha ka ili, a e lilo aku ana keia aina ma lalo o Kahiki."[16]

[Kala'ikuahulu is the one who said . . . "I am going to die, but if you folks live and if a canoe of priests, named Kahikimakalike, arrives from the sea, then grasp it and hold fast to it, for there will be a priest for you. Your skin will not be hurt [as in battle] and this land will one day be controlled by Kahiki."]

This prophecy was said to have been uttered before a chiefess named Ka'ahumanu and her sisters. Ka'ahumanu, a prominent figure in Hawai'i's history and wife of the well-known Kamehameha I, was born in the 1700s, in precontact Hawai'i, or what Kealani Cook refers to as "Ka Wā 'Ōiwi Wale."[17]

She then died in the mid-1800s a converted Christian, having "grasped" and "held fast" to the new "priest."

While we cannot know how Kalaʻikuahulu's words were interpreted by Kaʻahumanu and her sisters, the writers of *Ka Nupepa Kuokoa* state, "A o ua Kahiki la, o Amerika Huipua [As for this Kahiki just mentioned, it is the United States of America]."[18] Given the political context of the time in which the article was published, and the fact that this particular newspaper (despite its name meaning "The Independent Newspaper") was "a site for colonizing discourses," this interpretation of "Kahiki" makes sense.[19] It was printed in April 1893, just a few short months after the illegal overthrow of the Hawaiian Kingdom. Although interpretations like this complicate our understanding of Kahiki, they demonstrate the ability of each generation to add to this concept, shifting its meanings to accommodate new times. We may not always sit well with past interpretations and applications of Kahiki. However, we cannot escape their place in our histories, and cannot deny the fact that any discomfort we may feel about Kahiki being used to perhaps justify colonialism is only in retrospect, based largely on who we are and what we know *now*. We cannot fault our kūpuna, in other words, for what we believe was the right way or the right choice. We will never know what they experienced. Thus, we can only learn from them.

In my initial exploration of Kahiki, I gravitated toward older meanings, particularly those that seemed to celebrate a homeland based in the Pacific. Contemporarily, it was a concept that I and other Kānaka Maoli could use to reaffirm our relationships with other islands and islanders. It was a means of combating notions of our worlds as being small, limited, or isolated and was a vehicle toward what Epeli Hauʻofa calls "world enlargement."[20] In my early research, therefore, I focused intently on Kahiki as being that genealogical link that could both enlarge our worlds and expand our notions of self. I saw it as a means of cultivating hope, of reconnecting to the region and therefore celebrating the many routes that our ancestors traveled and the many paths that we can continue to travel as we work our ways back to each other, and in the process, toward the betterment of our Pacific peoples and places.

Problematically, however, in focusing so closely on the positive opportunities that Kahiki provided, especially in regard to reconnection, I suspended criticism, even of myself. I neglected to understand, for instance, that my personal use of the term "Kahiki" had limits, and that, unless used carefully, it promoted a relationship with the rest of the region that was far too slack to be of true benefit to those I used it to refer to. The potential danger of a word like "Kahiki" is that it can become another umbrella term that flattens a region that is incredibly diverse and that resists any attempt to define it clearly. (Kahiki's very history, after all, is one of conflation.) Furthermore, if I am honest about my prior interactions in and with the Pacific, they were largely based in Polynesia. Thus, when I spoke about "Kahiki" and about ancestral connections, I may have *referred* to the larger region while only truly *acting* upon, or embodying, my relationships with specific parts of it. When my student challenged the effectiveness of solidarity statements, I began to question what and who was included in my prior references to Kahiki, and wondered, quite critically, how some of our relationships in the Pacific, while attempting to subvert colonial powers, may actually be facilitated by them, thereby reinforcing the centrality of their role in our lives.

Ka Hiki, Arriving at Relationships

Before speaking about relationships with Kahiki, it would be remiss of me to not acknowledge the fact that Kahiki is not used in everyday discourse. In fact, as I will discuss at length in chapter 4, although Kahiki holds a prominent place in our narratives of migration, it is not always present in our contemporary articulations of identity as Kānaka Maoli, especially as roots take priority over routes in struggles for Indigenous rights. The knowledge of having genealogical relations in the Pacific is indeed present. However, it is not always acknowledged by name and not always brought forward, especially in contexts where "firstness" must be emphasized in struggles for land and space. With such an admission, therefore, one might wonder why I choose to place so much emphasis on it, centralizing it, and calling it back from the corners of our memories to a place where it can be reactivated and reinvigorated. If the name Kahiki is not part of dominant conversations now, to put it simply, does it have to be?

When I began researching Kahiki years ago as a PhD student, I found value in it being a possible avenue toward acting upon Hauʻofa's charge that we develop a "substantial regional identity that is anchored in our common inheritance of a very considerable portion of Earth's largest body of water, the Pacific Ocean."[21] In his influential essay "The Ocean in Us," he called upon people of Oceania to embrace a regional identity not to replace other identities but to enable us to work together for our collective interests, particularly in regard to safeguarding our lands, waters, and oceans. This identity, he argued, was needed to sustain trends in the Pacific to "move from mere protests to the stage of active protection of the environment."[22] I therefore believe that Kahiki is useful in reminding Kānaka Maoli of our shared belonging and shared responsibility to the rest of the Pacific (and that it can also serve as a prompting for other islanders to use their own Indigenous or ancestral concepts to remember as well). At the same time, it is a reminder that belonging is complex, and that in seeking to claim and maintain a regional identity we must be open to self-critique and to considering how and why our relationships in the Pacific are formed, why they are maintained (or not), and further, the potential impacts that claiming a regional identity can have, especially as islanders are increasingly mobile and find themselves/ourselves in each other's spaces.

Relationships, as Manulani Meyer suggests, "are not nouns, they are *verbs* . . . . Relationship as verb infers the *intentional quality* of connection that is *experienced* and remembered."[23] In regard to Kahiki, therefore, I see it as an opportunity to remember our ancestral connections in order to engage in the labor of not only fostering and strengthening relationships but of also holding ourselves accountable to them. The potential of Kahiki as a space for doing so is embedded in its name. Kahiki is comprised of two root words, "ka," a definite singular article usually translated simply as "the," and "hiki," which has various meanings, thereby leaving "Kahiki" open to multiple interpretations. To "hiki" is to arrive, to arise, to appear, or to reach a particular location, whether physical or not. The word "hiki" can also be used to indicate that something is possible or that it can be done.[24] Thus, "ka hiki" can refer to the arrival or the arising of someone or something. At the same time, it can also refer to ability and possibility. This one name, therefore, caries not only the power of an ancestral homeland and the knowledge of our connection to it but also of the opportunities and the potential we have to emerge, rise, and "arrive" back at each other in meaningful ways. Thus, I propose that in contemporary movements, including efforts to protect our environments, it would be useful to see Kahiki not so much as a name but as an action, or as the invitation to investigate how we connect, via both similarities and differences, and what is produced in our coming together. Taiaiake Alfred explains that in many Indigenous languages the names that people are given are often not just references or titles but responsibilities that imply doing.[25] Kahiki, therefore, is the space to *do*, or to act upon our memories of relation.

We must acknowledge, of course, the incredible amount of connections that have already been established and that are being continuously nurtured between different island groups and between different individuals in the Pacific. The expressions of love and support being shared between protectors at Ihumātao and Mauna Kea, for instance, is one recent example. Decades before this, as both Hauʻofa and more recently, Tracey Banivanua-Mar, have discussed, Pacific peoples came together to fight for a nuclear-free Pacific, meeting at a conference in Fiji in 1975 and later mobilizing and acting upon their mission in the 1980s and '90s to end nuclear testing in the region.[26] Banivanua-Mar also talks about the Pohnpei Charter, a "radical document" created in 1978 that "invoked 'the rights of indigenous peoples' against 'the degrading influences of Imperialism and Colonialism.'"[27] The charter was a result of representatives from Aotearoa, Hawaiʻi, New Caledonia, Tahiti, and Guåhan (Guam) meeting in Pohnpei, in what is now the Federated States of Micronesia, to discuss how they could protect the region together. The acceptance of regional connections can also be seen in cultural renaissance movements, particularly in the revival of noninstrument navigation and wayfinding in Polynesia, which will be discussed in chapter 4. It can also be seen in festivals such as the Festival of Pacific Arts, held every four years at a different location in Oceania. Additionally, in Aotearoa, there is increasing acceptance of a "Pasifika" or "Pasefika" identity, especially for New Zealand–born Pacific peoples who find strength in embracing a sense of belonging to a larger community that links their individual families and ethnic groups together in the diaspora.[28] There is no shortage of examples to highlight transregional connections and the willingness to nurture relationships and Pacific identities in Oceania. My goal in critically examining relationships, therefore, is to revisit how it is that we "arrive" *to* and *at* our relationships with one another so that we can be more conscious of what brings us together and why our meetings matter. It is also to interrogate our current connections to reveal the gaps and silences. Who are we *not* speaking to, who are we *not* including, which issues are *not* being addressed, and, in short, what "arrivals" and opportunities are we putting off (or not aware of) and why?

Paying Attention to Crossings

In returning to my student's question about solidarity, the list of hashtags referenced in our class discussion included Hawai'i, Aotearoa, Australia, and West Papua. What these places have in common is the fact that they are all settler colonies, though in the case of Hawai'i and West Papua, we could say that they are both under illegal military occupation with what J. Kēhaulani Kauanui describes as an "overlay" of settler colonialism.[29] Before progressing, I should note that Australia is not usually regarded as "Pacific" and is therefore not often addressed as a central focus in Pacific studies. Thus, it was brought into the conversation by students because of the struggles of the Indigenous peoples there and *not* because of its position in Oceania. This distinction is important, as it reveals networks between Indigenous peoples in the region and those outside of it. In the case of these four places and the issues they face, finding the points of connection is a means of bringing them together, and for those of us involved in these struggles, a means of finding our ways to each other.

After returning from Mauna Kea, I was asked to visit Ihumātao, to speak on behalf of the kia'i at Pu'uhonua o Pu'uhuluhulu, and to give the protectors there our love and support. While I traveled to Ihumātao, a contingent of Māori from Aotearoa traveled to Mauna Kea. We synched our arrivals so that our exchanges of support could happen at the same time, across our ocean. As documented in an article in *Te Ao Māori News*, I said, "Mauna Kea and Ihumātao are not isolated moments, they are movements that speak to each other across oceans . . . from Mauna Kea, we recognize the struggle at Ihumātao because we know it, we've felt it. From Mauna Kea, we've also felt the Māori recognition of our struggle, we've felt the prayers, we've been inspired by the actions, and we've been empowered by the solidarity."[30] In my own statements, I brought two peoples and places together, recognizing that we had similar experiences, both knowing the weight of settler colonialism, and what it feels like to be Indigenous while your lands, waters, culture, and identity are constantly threatened. My goal in going to Ihumātao and in offering a few words on the whenua was not to ignore specific contexts and key differences, or to compare and contrast, but to see how we could uplift one another, building on what united us. Further, on a very personal level, it was to practice what my students and I discuss: being an intellectual willing to visibly represent a viewpoint, despite any and all backlash, and to engage in embodied, experienced, and relational activism. My sharing of this story is not at all to congratulate myself, or to feel better about myself, which is one of the primary critiques of slacktivism, or to highlight my own actions over those of other protectors. Rather, it is to point to (and demonstrate) the ways that Kahiki can help us consider our activism and our relationships critically.

Kahiki, as explained earlier, can be framed as a sanctuary, a place to visit for safety and protection as well as a space for growth, or for learning from deep assessment and reflection. Additionally, "ka hiki" implies that there is opportunity and potential to "arrive" at new ways of thinking about colonialism, decolonization, regionalism, and unity in the region. Therefore, in considering my own solidarity work in the context of my students' presentations and comments in class, I have to implicate myself, recognizing not only the benefits of my work but the potential drawbacks of it as well. My own movement from one place to another, traveling across and between Ihumātao and Mauna Kea, can be described, to borrow a term from Chadwick Allen, as "trans-Indigenous."[31] In his articulation of methodologies for Indigenous literary studies, Allen points to the traps of comparative frameworks, particularly when "Indigenous-to-Indigenous comparison recenters the (uninformed) dominant settler culture and produces hierarchies of Indigenous oppression."[32] These hierarchies have been perpetuated in some of my students' responses when they compare their own struggles to those being experienced in places like West Papua and conclude that they should stop complaining about their own lives, stating that it could have been worse. Such attitudes, unfortunately, can preclude action for their peoples. To avoid the problematics of comparison, Allen therefore suggests a trans-Indigenous approach to studying literature that can provide space for accommodating and accounting for "contingent asymmetry and the potential risks of unequal encounters."[33]

Allen's methodology for literary analysis is also helpful in considering the movement of Indigenous peoples in the region and the complexities of our crossing into, through, and between each other's spaces. Describing Allen's work, Hōkūlani Aikau, Noelani Goodyear-Kaʻōpua, and Noenoe

Silva explain that the term "trans-Indigenous" "urges us to pay attention to the process of crossing from one context to another and to see what such crossings tell us."[34] In an interview coinciding with the 2019 Native American and Indigenous Studies Association conference held in Waikato, Aotearoa, Tēvita O. Ka'ili described trans-Indigeneity as "the idea that as indigenous people are moving outside of their homeland, they are in contact with other indigenous people . . . . And so it's sort of the collaborative work that they're doing, the sort of co-operation that's happening with multiple indigenous."[35] There is much to be learned and gained in investigating the movement "between" and "through" that comparative frames simply do not allow opportunity for. As both a space for reflection and the opportunity to act upon our relationships, Kahiki can support and align with the goals of trans-Indigeneity, providing opportunity to learn from the movements, interactions, and expressions between and across groups of Pacific peoples. Additionally, rather than trying to group people together in shallow (and often detrimental) ways, it can encourage collaboration and working together while also acknowledging diversity.

In paying close attention to the process of crossing, and what is produced in that crossing, however, we must also be aware of the gaps and silences. While the support being expressed and enacted between Ihumātao and Mauna Kea can be labeled as trans-Indigenous, I must ask myself if trans-Indigeneity is applicable to *all* parts of the region, and perhaps more importantly, if it should be. Recalling the four places represented previously in hashtag form—Hawai'i, Aotearoa, Australia, and West Papua—each has Indigenous peoples. In settler colonial contexts, being called "Indigenous" has specific purpose and meaning. The term's use, in other words, is intentional. While there is no one agreed-upon definition of "Indigenous"—as attempts to define it should come from the people the term is being applied to and should be unique to place—it is helpful to look at some of the commonalities between Indigenous peoples. In the often-referenced study by José Martínez Cobo, Indigenous communities and nations are described as "those which, having a historical continuity with preinvasion and precolonial societies that, developed on their territories, consider themselves distinct from other sectors of the societies now prevailing in those territories, or parts of them. They form at present non-dominant sectors of society and are determined to preserve, develop and transmit to future generations their ancestral territories, and their ethnic identity, as the basis of their continued existence as peoples, in accordance with their own cultural patterns, social institutions and legal systems."[36] Further, the United Nations Working Group on Indigenous Populations listed one of the factors relevant in understanding "Indigenous" as "an experience of subjugation, marginalization, dispossession, exclusion or discrimination, whether or not these conditions persist."[37] Using this understanding, the first peoples of Hawai'i, Aotearoa,

Australia, and West Papua can be categorized as "Indigenous." They/We are "non-dominant sectors of society," or are quickly becoming so in the case of West Papua and mass transmigration from Indonesia.[38] Additionally, we are committed to what Michael Chandler calls "persistent indigeneity," or continuing to experience ourselves as Indigenous to ensure that our future generations can do the same.[39]

Due to these associations with the term "Indigenous," not all Pacific Islanders identify themselves as such, and not all want to. In her influential work *Decolonizing Methodologies: Research and Indigenous Peoples*, Linda Tuhiwai Smith explains that "Indigenous" is a term that emerged from, and found purpose in, the struggles of colonized peoples, gaining momentum in the 1970s: "The term has enabled the collective voices of colonized people to be expressed strategically in the international arena. It has also been an umbrella enabling communities and peoples to come together, transcending their own colonized contexts and experiences, in order to learn, share, plan, organize and struggle collectively for self-determination on the global and local stages."[40] Thus, in our trans-Indigenous efforts in the Pacific region, are we using an umbrella term that does not fit all and/or are we limiting our relationships to only those who experience themselves as Indigenous? If the latter is true, are we thereby allowing our relationships to be facilitated by shared experiences of struggle at the hands of colonizing powers, thus (re)centralizing them and enabling them to affect how and why we come together (or not) as Pacific peoples? As a Kanaka Maoli, and as someone who identifies as Indigenous, I've always felt comfortable using the term and have often used it quite casually in the region to refer to anyone of Pacific Island descent. In coming to Kahiki, however, I've had to rethink my relationships with Pacific peoples and admit that in my own efforts to draw connections I also conflated "Indigenous" and "Pacific" in detrimental ways.

In her exploration of Taiwan-Tuvalu cultural diplomacy, Jess Marinaccio problematizes this all-too-common conflation, arguing that the assumption that *all* Pacific Islanders understand themselves as Indigenous fails "to account for understandings of indigeneity in the independent Pacific."[41] In an interview, Marinaccio recorded the former Kiribati ambassador as saying, quite simply and pointedly, "For us, there's really no other race to say that we are the indigenous people, you know?"[42] In the independent Pacific, in other words, where islanders *are* the majority and are not being pushed out or erased by settler colonies, there may be both no use for the term "Indigenous" and no desire to be grouped together with those who use it. For some, "Indigenous" implies defeat, dispossession, and erasure. For others, "Indigenous" is like an "indelible stain," marking you and your people as lost or losing.[43] Thus, when we lay our terms and names onto others, we risk erasing their experiences of themselves and replacing them with our own.

These problems and questions must be raised in assessing our work in the Pacific and in reflecting back on the unfair homogenizing that may come from our attempts, however well-intentioned, to strengthen a regional identity and to act for one another. While I support the goals, intentions, and incentives of trans-Indigeneity, particularly as it encourages us to move away from "vertical Indigenous-settler (nation-state) relations" and toward "lateral Indigenous connections . . . [and] the possibility of center-to-center conversations about Indigenous Nations," I am also wary of what this can mean in the Pacific.[44] First, if we apply this term to people who do not use it themselves, are we allowing space for the diversity of experiences and the range of ways it is to be and know oneself as "Pacific"? Secondly, if our most salient connections are between those who've struggled in similar ways, do we risk promoting and perpetuating colonial boundaries imposed on the region and, further, once again centralizing the role of those colonial powers in closing us off to each other? Finally, to return to my student's concern about solidarity, if we bring peoples and experiences together to speak to the larger issues of colonization, dispossession, and ongoing subjugation, can we unconsciously place so much emphasis on the ways that we relate that we neglect the necessary work of unpacking all of the ways we are different?

Kahiki as Sanctuary

In taking myself to Kahiki, or to a space for sitting in the discomfort of examining our relationships in new ways, I cannot ignore the fact that "Indigenous" is but one of many terms and concepts that we must consider critically when we look at how and why we come together. In other words, while exposing some of the difficulties in using a term like "Indigenous," it would be irresponsible of me to not also acknowledge that the terms I've been using in this chapter—and in this book as a whole—are also problematic and limiting. "Pacific" and "Oceania," for instance are introduced terms. In one of my Pacific studies classes, PASI 101: The Pacific Heritage, we look at the meanings of the word "pacific" and discuss how definitions such as "peaceful," "idyllic," "calm," and "tranquil" have actually become the lens through which some of our islands and islanders are now perceived. In Hawai'i, Haunani-Kay Trask probably described the effects of these perceptions best when she wrote about the tourism industry selling the idea that "everything in Hawai'i can be yours."[45] The assumption is that we are always welcoming, always accommodating, and always happy. Though some of my students do not realize it at first, they come to understand the power of names and how a term like "pacific" can be damaging. In his seminal essay "Our Sea of Islands," Hau'ofa advocated for the term "Oceania" over "Pacific," arguing that "*Oceania* denotes a sea of islands with their inhabitants," thus not only emphasizing scale and mass—thereby combating notions of smallness—but

also the seaways that connect us as Pacific peoples.[46] Though this is com-
pelling, the name "Pacific" endures, even in my own writing. Other names
that endure include those of the three subregions of the Pacific: Polynesia,
Melanesia, and Micronesia. These terms, also introduced, have racist under-
pinnings and have separated islands and islanders as much as they've sought
to connect us.

As I sit in Kahiki, I have to hold myself accountable and admit that I
continue to use these terms because they've become entrenched in the region.
While this does not make them any less problematic, I use them because
they've become part of us and, like Kahiki, can be changed. When I talk to
my students, for example, especially those of Pacific Island descent who were
born and raised in Aotearoa, "Pacific" is a name they use for themselves and
is one that enables them to find ways to connect to other Pacific peoples who
may not share their same ethnic background but who know the experience
of living away from their ancestral homelands. "Pacific," for them, can be
empowering. Similarly, although Polynesia, Micronesia, and Melanesia come
from racist assumptions made by early European explorers, islanders have
also adopted them and in many ways claimed the right to mold them. In the
region known as Melanesia, for example, Tarcisius Kabutaulaka explains that
"Melanesians have now appropriated the term 'Melanesia' and are using it to
challenge the negative representations—to 're-present' and 'alter' the images
of Melanesia."[47] This adoption and appropriation of the name can also be
heard in music coming from the region that promotes a Melanesian identity
while sometimes even celebrating the "mela."[48]

The continued use of these names in the Pacific, however, is often challenged (as it should be). In fact, taking Hau'ofa's arguments a step further,
some Pacific scholars have advocated for the use of "Moana" over "Oceania":
"Moana [meaning "ocean" in some Pacific languages], they say, identifies the
entire Pasifika people, their lands, their waters and their cultures."[49] Similar
to the often-uncritical use of the term "Indigenous," however, "Moana" presents its own problems. Julia Mage'au Gray, who was born Papua New Guinea,
for example, critiqued the attempt to find one word to speak for the entire
Pacific, especially when Papua New Guinea alone has over eight hundred
languages and Melanesia is one of the most linguistically diverse regions in
the world. She called the attempt "a very Western idea" and explained that for
some Papua New Guineans who live far from the coast, "Moana doesn't really
mean a lot."[50] As a term coming from various Polynesian languages, "Moana"
can pose the same threat that "Indigenous" does if not used carefully. It can,
in other words, erase cultural distinctiveness even while it seeks to honor it,
creating a name for the region while simultaneously pushing aside some of
those it is meant to represent.

I raise these issues here, at the end of this chapter, to serve as an example of some of the considerations that must be made in examining our

relationships. When my student asked about solidarity—who we speak for, why we try to do so, and the potential pitfalls of our well-intentioned efforts—he encouraged me to reflect on slackness. Sometimes, even while we engage in difficult, draining, and emotionally heavy struggles for our peoples, we can become lazy in some of the words and strategies we use. Thus, I am left wondering if part of Tagi Qolouvaki's encouragement to engage in "mana-full" resistance that is "decolonial, contagious, and muscled" was to get us to not only unravel the effects of colonialism but also realize when we become complicit in those effects, presenting them in new guises. Once you start to unravel colonial legacies, the undoing catches. The first question leads to many more. The first realization leads to subsequent ones. Finally, the first effort to carry the burden of working through the complexities of our region, our peoples, our many identities, and our futures leads to our minds and bodies being conditioned, and muscled, to keep on going.

3

WHAT IS BELOW SHALL RISE

Kahiki and Radical Hope

While at Puʻuhonua o Puʻuhuluhulu in July of 2019, I gathered with kiaʻi every day, three times a day, for ceremony. We chanted to greet the elements, danced to honor prominent deities, prayed for the protection of our mountain, and called for the restoration of ea: life, breath, and sovereignty. Among the chants and dances that were part of the daily ritual was an old wānana, or prophecy, that foretells reversal: E iho ana ʻo luna, e piʻi ana ʻo lalo, e hui ana nā moku, e kū ana ka paia. What is up shall come down, what is below shall rise, the islands will unite, the walls will stand. First uttered by a famous kāula, or prophet, named Kapihe in the early 1800s, this prophecy has since become central in Kanaka Maoli movements calling for a restoration of justice, an overturning of colonial structures that continue to oppress, an ending of destruction and desecration, and a return of Kānaka to ʻāina. It has been used to express dissatisfaction with the status quo and hope, however radical, for a different future. While standing to protect Mauna Kea, it was (and is) a statement of strength, one lifted to the summit of the mountain, every day, multiple times a day, expressing our dedication and our unwavering commitment.

I first learned to recite this wānana as a chant when I was a young girl standing in prayer and protest circles, my voice being led by my cousin and kumu hula, Pua Case. As I grew, the chant grew with me, accompanying me when I traveled with family to different events, whether to march with thousands on the streets of Honolulu in 1998 to mark the one hundredth year since the illegal annexation of Hawai'i,[1] or to smaller, more intimate spaces, praying for change. In my final year of high school, I attended a new and revolutionary charter school, Kanu o ka 'Āina. Grounded in Hawaiian culture, beliefs, and values, we ended every single day by chanting this prophecy, putting our voices together, lifting our collective hopes, and ending our chant declaring, "E ulu nā kanu o ka 'āina," "Let the children of the land grow and prosper." It was our daily affirmation and our daily commitment to do what we could, even as students, to ensure that we would always have a place in this world, even if the world was (and still is), as Michael Chandler states bluntly, "no longer willing to make a place" for us.[2]

Though used in an optimistic and visionary way today, however, this prophecy was not always embraced. In fact, it was sometimes challenged. Kapihe, the one who first uttered the wānana, was once described by Gideona La'anui as a "kanaka wahahee," or a lying, deceitful man, one with a mouth like that of a he'e, or octopus: slippery and slimy.[3] It is said that he offered his wānana in an era referred to as "Kanī'aukani," or the "Sounding of Coconut Ribs." This name was given to the time when the great chief Kamehameha I returned to the island of his birth. According to one account, he had spent nine years on the island of O'ahu and then set out in 1811 to return to Hawai'i Island.[4] It was following his return—in a time named for the sound that the chief's kāhili, or feathered standards, made in the wind while standing erect on his canoe—that Kapihe uttered his wānana.

In perhaps the earliest written record of Kapihe's prophecy, he is recorded as saying, "He huwi [hui] na moku, he ola na kupuna, he ihoiho ko luna o ka lani i lalo nei, he pii ae ko lalo nei i luna i ka lani, a he pi aku ka wai, peahi aku ka peahi, ola ka mai o ia la [The islands will unite, the ancestors will live, those in the sky above shall come down, those here below shall ascend into the sky, and the water will be sprinkled, the signal will be given, and the sick of today shall live]."[5] In his examination of the prophecy, John Charlot explains that because it was made *after* Kamehameha's unification of the Hawaiian Islands under one rule, "Kapihe's prophecy is one of the few surviving expressions of Hawaiian dissatisfaction with Kamehameha's reign."[6] Thus, La'anui—writing just twenty-seven or so years after Kapihe uttered those words—was quite hostile in his reaction toward the kāula. He was a supporter of Kamehameha who perhaps believed that "if Kapihe prophecies the *future* joining of the islands, he implies that somehow they have not yet been adequately unified by Kamehameha's conquests and reorganisation of the government."[7] Furthermore, the fall of those "in the sky," or those of higher rank, could have been read as the eventual collapse of Kamehameha's rule. Thus, Laʻanui was harsh in his criticism of the "kanaka wahahee," or the man with the slippery mouth.

Laʻanui's reaction, while critical, speaks to the power of Kapihe's prophecy. Despite disagreement and criticism, in other words, it has endured because it continues to find relevance. No matter how the wānana is interpreted, there seems to be an agreement that regardless of the situation it is being used to explain, there is an overarching anticipation of reversal, or of an overhaul of the way things currently are, whether positive or negative. Modern recitations of the chant call for what is up to come down and for what is below to rise. The ambiguity of these words is precisely what gives them their strength and what has contributed to the prophecy being brought from the time of Kanīʻaukani all the way to Puʻuhonua o Puʻuhuluhulu. Even while the words may shift to speak to different circumstances over time, the wānana reassures us that there will always be an opportunity for change, no matter how far-fetched such change may seem, and no matter the adversity that will undoubtedly come with it.

Through tracing the life of Kapihe's prophecy over time, this chapter will argue that wānana are sustained futurities, or the means to engage with the past in order to make our futures visible and knowable today. Futurities, as Laura Harjo describes, operate "in service to our ancestors, contemporary relatives, and future relatives" in the now.[3] A prophecy like Kapihe's, therefore, can function to bridge the unfulfilled desires of our kūpuna with our current actions and our attempts to create the conditions in which our future generations can continue to see their desires into fruition. In examining past and present engagements with this wānana, beginning in the nineteenth century—as Kānaka Maoli were writing, speaking, and debating their relationships with the outside world—and coming into our current movements, I hope to highlight historical agency. The life of Kapihe's prophecy, for instance, showcases the ability of our kūpuna to use ancestral knowledge in ways that suited their political agendas, regardless of what they were and whether or not we agree with them today. The different versions of the prophecy, including one that speaks about uniting with "Kahiki," reflect how they were engaging, experiencing, and explaining their changing worlds, thus leaving us with both a genealogy of ideas and the opportunity to add to it. In this chapter, Kahiki will be framed as a sanctuary, or as a safe and sustained space for imagining alternative futures, then and now. In utilizing Kahiki in this way, I hope this chapter will also push us to consider Pacific futurities and our radical hopes and actions for the region.

Prophesizing Futures

One afternoon at Puʻuhonua o Puʻuhuluhulu, directly after our noon ceremony, a man was called forward to share a few words with the kiaʻi. Grabbing the microphone and standing before the kūpuna seated in the shade of their tent and the rest of us gathered around, he spoke about Kapihe's prophecy. He recited the words and explained them line by line, tying their meaning back to what brought all of us together: our dedication to Mauna Kea and our commitment to protect it. His words were passionate and encouraging. When he was finished, he had us chant the wānana one more time, this time with more conviction and hope. Those who did not know the meaning of the prophecy beforehand were able to do it with new vigor, their chanting no longer a simple recitation but a declaration of what they wanted for the future.

When we were done, I sat down with my mom, thinking and talking about Kapihe. The explanation given for his wānana was an inspiring one, one framed by and for our struggles for sovereignty. While this is what I focus my thoughts on, or what I direct my energy to while chanting, I believe that each time Kapihe's prophecy is delivered, we also recite a history, one that was not always so positive and encouraging. Though we may not always want to acknowledge older versions and interpretations of the prophecy, or the fact that its first utterance may have been in disapproval of one of our most famous and beloved chiefs (especially on the Big Island of Hawai'i, where he was from), I believe that our contemporary use of his wānana is more potent not in spite of its complicated history but because of it. Each time we chant and call for reversal, in other words, we can also find strength in knowing that we are doing what our ancestors did before us: using these same words to speak to our own times and shifting circumstances. Like our kūpuna, and even like the brave kāula before us, we are not only prophesizing futures but also creating them and calling them to us with every word. Thus, even while I have wondered where and who our contemporary prophets are today, chanting on the mauna made me realize that there is a bit of kāula in all of us.

Being Kapihe

Each time we chant Kapihe's words, we become like him. Though his words may not have always been seen as positive, they enable us to see into a future and to voice what we desire for it. This is what I would call an expression of "radical hope." "What makes this hope *radical*," according to Jonathan Lear, "is that it is directed toward a future goodness that transcends the current ability to understand what it is."[9] When I first read Lear's work, I latched on to this idea, believing that it explained how and why I could have hope for my people, our lands, our waters, our culture, and our futures, even when the world left me with very little to justify that hope. When your life is full of examples that point to collapse, for instance, it can be difficult to maintain faith in a future that will be any different or that will somehow move in another direction. The daily bombardment of news about Indigenous peoples struggling around the world to save their/our homes, their/our sacred spaces, and their/our rights to exist as Indigenous are overwhelming. Every day, I am further troubled by the state of our planet and the refusal of world powers and powerful corporations to do anything to stop the rapid decline of our environments. It's heavy, and at times, it's all consuming. However, I firmly believe that no matter how "radical" or far-fetched and ridiculous it may seem, maintaining hope is my responsibility not only for us but also for those who have not yet been born. Having hope is radical because it helps us rise through and above the effects of the colonial "cultural bomb."[10] Along with attempting to annihilate our names, languages, cultures, beliefs, and core values, it also seeks to destroy our confidence in ourselves and our ability, our real ability, to change the course of history. When I chant Kapihe's prophecy, calling for what is above to fall and what is below to rise, I am calling for reversals that can and will change our world.

Recently, however, I've also realized the need to take my hope further, putting it into action. Writing about her experience and practice of being Mvskoke from Oklahoma, Harjo introduces the idea of "radical sovereignty." Though seeming to speak to something in the future, something not yet achieved, radical sovereignty happens in the now because, as she explained, it "does not have to wait for the nation-state to recognize it or deem it legitimate. Instead, it is embodied in being Mvskoke and practiced without permission from anyone."[11] For me, radical sovereignty is insisting on being Kānaka Maoli in practice, every day, unapologetically. Further, it is acting upon my hope not just in envisioning a better future but also in creating the conditions for that future now. Radical sovereignty is what some Kānaka Maoli do unconsciously, drawing on the knowledge and wisdom of our ancestors, acting in ways that do not depend on the settler state, or in some cases, even work to unsettle the state. It can be in everything from the seemingly banal activity of choosing Indigenous foods to the intentional and purposeful act of protest. Radical sovereignty is acting upon our hope, refusing the idea that we need permission to be who we are and refusing to be limited by state-imposed boundaries put on our visions for the future. It is to activate and embody futurities that decolonize our minds as well as to create "a future imaginary attentive to the past as it critiques the present, and ventures forward into the beyond."[12]

Looking at the history of Kapihe's wānana, I believe that those who engaged with it over time were also enacting futurities and using the wānana to do so. In the following section I will therefore trace some of this history of engagement: the prophecy's role in confronting changing circumstances, imagining what could come of those circumstances, and the role people could/would play in enabling their desired futures because of, or in spite of, their situations. In the nineteenth century, Kapihe's prophecy found its way into discussions about ancient customs, Christianity, the loss of land, and nationalism. Through time, it was interpreted as both a warning for the future, foreseeing collapse, and as a sign of hope, always depending on the author and their own political and social agendas in the times they lived. The history of Kapihe's prophecy in print, therefore, reveals how his words were never confined to the moments in which they were being expressed but instead spoke to futurity, or to creating in the present "that which our ancestors, we, and future relatives desire."[13]

Historical Agency

The life of this wānana began, as Laʻanui explains, when Kapihe recited his prophecy before a chief who had recently unified separate island chiefdoms under a single rule.[14] Other accounts of the time period known as Kanīʻaukani speak of how upon his return to Hawaiʻi Island, "Ua kukulu ae o ia i mau hale no na akua ona a me na kahu akua ona [Kamehameha built houses for his gods and for those who would take care of them]."[15] This included the "akua malihini," or the war gods of other islands that he had acquired in his conquests. Thus, Kapihe's prophesizing of "he ihoiho ko luna o ka lani i lalo nei, he pii ae ko lalo nei i luna i ka lani," or that those in the sky above will come down and that those here below will ascend into the sky, could have been read as a direct reflection of the elevated positioning of Kamehameha's many akua, or gods, and a foretelling of the fall of an entire belief system.

Just seven years after Kanīʻaukani came the end of the ʻaikapu, or the set of taboos that governed the political and spiritual lives of the people. As Samuel Kamakau explains, "He mea kupanaha, a he mea hiwahiwa lua ole ka hoohiolo ia ana o na kapu alii, na kapu akua, a me na kapu a na kahuna [The overthrow of the chiefly taboo, the godly taboo, and the taboo of the priests was a truly remarkable and incomparably astonishing event]."[16] Kamakau's choice of the word "hoʻohiolo" means that those old beliefs, including the physical and spiritual structures that Kamehameha erected for his gods, were made to "hiolo," or were made to tumble over, implying that there was conscious choice and action involved. Thus, what was up was indeed brought down, and it was the reversal of "those above" and "those below" that brought about significant change for Kānaka Maoli. What exactly comprised "ko luna," or that above, and "ko lalo," or that below, is subject to debate. In fact, according to Lilikalā Kameʻeleihiwa, the overthrow of the ʻaikapu "was not a conversion from Hawaiian *Akua* to the Christian *Akua*. It was a destruction of the old *Akua* in favor of nothing!"[17] In other words, it was not that the hoʻohiolo of the old beliefs and gods came with the immediate rise of Christianity, but rather that the ʻainoa (the name given to the time following the overthrow of the ʻaikapu, "noa" meaning "free of taboo") "created a kind of religious void" that Christianity could possibly—but not inevitably—come to fill.[18]

What's significant about this observation by Kameʻeleihiwa is that it enables us to view the past not as being fixed but as being flexible. If we do not see the "hoʻohiolo" as having only one inescapable result, in other words, we can untether our minds to consider alternative pasts, perhaps thinking about the other options our kūpuna had rather than to readily and wholly accept Christianity. This not only expands our understanding of history but also recognizes and honors historical agency, a concept I teach in one of our Pacific studies classes, PASI 201: Comparative History in Polynesia. Created by the late Teresia Teaiwa, this course enables students to engage with their histories, and the histories of the Polynesian region, in new ways.[19] Historical agency, as I explain it, "teaches students to consider the range of choices and actions possible in any given historical moment. It emphasizes the fact that our Pacific ancestors were not limited to the actions that we—as contemporary islanders with the privilege of hindsight—would like them to have chosen."[20] Thus, it teaches us to study the past and to acknowledge even those moments when our ancestors made choices that we may not agree with contemporarily, recognizing, first, that "they were not in a position to understand the significance of what it was they were about to endure" as a result of their choices, and second, that they were engaged in both trying to understand their present while also actively creating their future based on what they knew of the time.[21]

Being recorded and analyzed by Laʻanui in 1838, Kapihe's prophecy provided space for not only reflecting on the past and Kamehameha's actions as a naʻi aupuni, or "nation conqueror" but also on what happened after his reign, particularly with the ending of the ʻaikapu. Thus, the wānana and its ambiguity allowed for it to be used to explain changing circumstances and to point to, and act toward, an uncertain future. In fact, later renditions of Kapihe's prophecy reveal how Kānaka Maoli took advantage of his vague references to "that above" and "that below," using them to speak to the changes being witnessed after the introduction of Christianity and the possible place of these changes in their futures. In a version printed in 1860 the words of the famous wānana were changed, most notably to include reference to "ke Akua," or a single god, thus reflecting some of the changes that came with the fall of the ʻaikapu. The article, like Laʻanui's, also criticizes Kapihe—now representative of an old and unjust time—calling him "he pupule," or a crazy person. According to the account, Kapihe's prophecy is as follows:

E hui ana na aina	[The islands will unite
E iho mai ana ko ka lani	Those of above will come down
E pii aku ana ko lalo nei	Those of here below will rise up
E iho mai ana ke Akua i lalo nei	God will come down
E kamailio pu ana me kanaka	He will speak with the people
E pii mai ana o Wakea i luna	Wākea will rise up

E iho aku ana o Milo[22] i lalo   Milo will go down
E noho pu ana ke Akua me kanaka.   God will dwell with the people].[23]

What this 1860 recording reveals is that conversion to Christianity—despite its obvious influence—was not as successful as it sometimes appeared to be. While this rendering of the wānana does include a reference to "ke Akua," it also refers to Wākea and Milu, two figures that predate the arrival of foreigners. Wākea is often regarded as one of the first and oldest ancestors of the Hawaiian people. More than a progenitor, however, he also played a significant role in the creation of the universe. Wākea's domain was believed to be in the sky, while Milu was said to dwell in the underworld. Thus, the return of Wākea to the realm above and of Milu to the realm below could have been interpreted as a restoration of balance previously disrupted.[24]

Even with the obvious reference to Christian teachings, which perhaps influenced the way Kapihe's prophecy was recorded, traces of older belief systems could still be detected. In reading back and examining these historical texts it is therefore quite clear that Kānaka Maoli did not completely abandon their old beliefs and values. In fact, some Hawaiians "only partially accepted the new faith; only partially disavowed the old gods . . . . And some—even to this day—manage to believe in and accept both God and the *akua* [the many Hawaiian gods]."[25] This rendition of Kapihe's prophecy, therefore, was a futurity that sought to bridge the experiences of the past, the life of the present, and what was possible for the future: a balance of worlds and beliefs. This type of futurity was also witnessed in parts of Sāmoa where deliberately and publically destroying Samoan gods "was done not to show that ancestral Samoan spirits or powers were fictitious or imaginary, but in order to demonstrate the omnipotence of the Christian god."[26] In other words, islanders were not trying to deny the existence of older, Samoan gods but were merely making them inferior to the single Christian God. Thus, their many gods still had a space, albeit a lower one. Perhaps, as in the case of Hawai'i, this was a way of creating a future in which both could exist.

Futures in Kahiki

One year after this version was printed, a new rendition of Kapihe's prophecy appeared in the new independent Hawaiian language newspaper *Ka Hoku o ka Pakipika*. This version, like the 1860 recording, continues to combine Christian teachings with older beliefs. What is interesting, however, is the obvious increase in critical engagement with the prophecy. Whereas previous writers seemed to simply report on Kapihe's words, offering small comments and personal insights, the author of the 1861 version, Kauako'iawe, takes time to analyze it:

E iho mai ana ke akua e noho pu me kanaka, a e pii aku ana
hoi ko lalo nei i luna, a e hui ana hoi na pae moku mai Kahiki
a Hawaii nei i hookahi. Penei nae ka hoailona e hiki mai ai ma
mua: hookahi kanaha la e pouli ai; a laila, e ua mai ka ua, a kui ka
hekili, a olapa ka uwila, a pio mai hoi na anuenue ehiku. I laila e
ike aku ai kakou i ka poe make e ala mai ana mai na ilina mai, a
e ike aku kela kanaka keia kanaka i ko lakou poe makua, a me na
hoahanau i make e ma mua.[27]

[God will descend to dwell with the people, and those here below
will ascend, and the archipelagos, from Kahiki to Hawaiʻi, will
be united as one. This is the sign that will come before this: there
will be forty days of darkness, and then rain will fall, thunder will
crash, lightning will flash, and seven rainbows will appear arched.
It is then that we will see the dead rise from their graves, and each
person will see his or her parents and relatives who passed on
before.]

Aside from being much longer than previous versions—and the fact that
Kauakoʻiawe places Kapihe's prophecy *before* Kamehameha's unification of
the islands—his rendition also includes new elements. Whereas Laʻanui's
account spoke of the eventual unification of "moku," or islands, and the
1860 version used the term "ʻāina," or land, Kauakoʻiawe's article speaks of
"pae moku," or archipelagos. Adding to the complexity of his account—and
deepening my own intrigue—is the fact that he attempts to include specifics,
saying that lands from Kahiki to Hawaiʻi will be as one.

Kahiki, as past scholarship has indicated, is not a specific location.[28]
Rather, as explored in previous parts of this book, it is the concept of a Pacific
homeland; it is the very idea of origin and is often celebrated as the place
where our ancestors came from, the place where life began, and the place
that continues to sustain life in Hawaiʻi long after settlement in the islands.
Over time, however, "Kahiki" changed to meet new times, becoming a term
used to refer to *all* places beyond Hawaiʻi's shores, even those with colonial
interests. In some cases, it was even used in reference to, both simply and
perplexingly, "all that is distant in time and space."[29] Thus, Kauakoʻiawe's
inclusion of Kahiki is interesting as it simultaneously draws upon genealogy
and being connected, or reconnected, to an ancestral homeland in Oceania,
while also suggesting relationships with everything beyond the Pacific. The
shift in Kahiki's meaning and application, becoming much more broad
and expansive, was evident in Kauakoʻiawe's analysis of Kapihe's prophecy.
Despite the clear use of "pae moku," which is a group of islands and not a
continent, Kauakoʻiawe draws on later interpretations of "Kahiki," which
by that time was commonly used to refer to any land outside of Hawaiʻi,

continents included.[30] In reference to Kahiki, he states, "Ua hui hoi na aupuni
kanaka i hookahi, mai Amelika, a me na aina ano kanaka e ae; eia pu me
kakou [Other nations of people, from America and other inhabited places,
have become as one; they are here with us]."[31] In his interpretation of Kapihe's
words, therefore, the unification of Kahiki and Hawai'i was fulfilled with the
arrival of Americans and other foreigners.

If I examined this particular version of Kapihe's prophecy without
Kauako'iawe's analysis, I could have easily assumed that his wānana (as re-
produced in this article) was referring to the eventual unification of archipelagos in the Pacific, from Kahiki to Hawai'i. In fact, in retrospect, this
version could appear to support a stance of resistance against American encroachment, foretelling the rise of Kānaka Maoli and their joining together
with their Pacific relations. However, looking back from a particular "van-
tage point," as Isabel Hofmeyr argues, can obscure the conditions in which
the text was initially produced, thereby denying those who produced it their
agency.[32] Furthermore, to view the text through the lens of resistance can
privilege contemporary voices and ideas over those of the past. It would be
dishonest of me to not admit that I have been guilty of this: of searching for
resistance, or of searching for something to make contemporary Hawaiians
feel righteous. In doing so, however, I created an overlay of colonial refusal,
and subsequently, obscured the past. In exploring the complex engagements
and entanglements with Kahiki over time, however, I have learned that rather
than trying to strategically sidestep those moments in history that may not
align with my current political views, it would be far more generative to get
closer to them, acknowledging the multiple paths that people have taken and
recognizing the effects that drastically different circumstances had on their
thinking, choices, and actions, whether we agree with them or not. Reading
these historical texts and trying to understand them in the contexts in which
they were created is critical. It requires looking back through the minds of
those who wrote them, no matter how difficult it may be, so that we can begin
to understand what some Kānaka Maoli were thinking and feeling about the
times in which they lived.

Kauako'iawe was not the only one to use the wānana to instigate necessary discussions about Hawai'i's future. In 1897, one year before the illegal
annexation of Hawai'i to the United States, a brief conversation about "Na
Wanana i Hooko ia," or "Prophecies That Have Been Fulfilled," appeared
between two newspapers, commenting on the role of "Kahiki," which in this
case was America. The first article was printed in *Ke Aloha Aina*, a paper
started by Joseph Nāwahī, who was a staunch opponent of annexation and
a firm "aloha 'āina," or patriot. It was in this paper, one named for patriotism to the Hawaiian Nation, that the discussion of wānana began with an
article written by Nā Kia'i o ka Pō, or the Guardians of the Night.[33] These
kia'i list a series of prophecies made in the "wā kahiko" (ancient times) and

then provide evidence of their fulfillment. In their version, Kapihe's wānana is as follows: "Ke hoea aela, a ke nalo ihola, a ke nalowale loa akula, ke pii aela ko lalo, a ke iho ihola ko luna [Arriving, passing, disappearing, what is below is rising, and what is above is coming down]."[34] In reflecting on this prophecy first uttered in the time of Kamehameha, they state, "Ua hooko keia wanana ma muli o ka nalowale ana o ke Aupuni Moi Hawaii i ka 1893. Elua, ke pii aela ko lalo, ke iho ihola ko luna, ua hooko ia ma ke kaili ia ana o ka noho alii mai ka noho Moiwahine ana o Liliuokalani, a pii aela ka makaain-ana lopa a lilo i Peresidena [This prophecy was fulfilled with the loss of the Hawaiian Nation in 1893. Secondly, in terms of that of below rising and that of above coming down, this was fulfilled with the seizing of the throne from Liliʻuokalani's reign, and the advancement of a peasant commoner to the role of president]."[35]

While the kiaʻi admit that Kānaka Maoli have suffered great loss, they conclude with hope: "Ua make ka lahui, ke alii, a me ka aina, ua like me ka make o ke kalo. Aka, ua ola hou no ma kekahi ano [The nation, the chiefs, and the land have been defeated, like the perishing of the kalo (taro). But, it lives anew in some ways]."[36] In response to their radical hope and their asser-tion that their people would continue to live, albeit differently, another article was published in *Ka Nupepa Kuokoa*, a newspaper dedicated to the "coloniz-ing project."[37] Written by Nā Kiaʻi o ke Ao, or the Guardians of the Light, the article, "Ahea la pau ke kuhihewa o ka lahui," or "When will the erroneous suppositions of the nation be over?" goes through each wānana listed by Nā Kiaʻi o ka Pō, giving the authors' assessments and reactions. The deliberate choice of name here is quite telling. Pō and ao are complementary opposites. According to Kealani Cook, "pō" could refer to "the night, generic dark-ness, and the time/being that was the primordial darkness . . . [which] came before anything else and birthed the rest of the universe," while "ao" "could mean light, daytime, the temporal world and/or the present post-Pō era."[38] Like other terms, however, "pō" and "ao" were heavily Christianized and had therefore taken on new meanings. "Pō" was used to represent the pre-Christian, pagan and uncivilized era, and "ao" was used to represent a time of enlightenment. Given their nationalistic stance, Nā Kiaʻi o ka Pō could have been looking at older understandings of "pō" as a place of birth, creation, and rebirth. As revealed in their response, Nā Kiaʻi o ke Ao, on the other hand, stood for newer understandings of "ao" as a space of "civilization."

In reference to Kapihe's prophecy, Nā Kiaʻi o ke Ao state, "Pololei oe [You are correct]."[39] In other words, they agree that the words of this famous kāula were fulfilled with the loss of the nation and the seizure of the government in 1893. What they disagree with, however, are their feelings about it. As obvi-ous supporters of annexation, the "Guardians of the Light" try to persuade readers to not be swayed by the resistance of the aloha ʻaina, and then record the words of two sisters whose sentiments they use to push their own agenda:

Pane aela kekahi wahine aloha aina: "Aole au e make a noho hou
ka Moiwahine ma ka noho Moi." Eia ka pane a kona kaikaina, he
hoohui aina oiaio: "E make e ana ia a me a'u, aole loa e hoi hou ae
ka Moiwahine ma ka noho Moi." Ke manaoio nei au o ka pane a
ke kaikaina ka pane pololei. Na'u no e kiola aku i na alii mai ko
lakou mau noho alii ae.[40]

[One woman patriot responded: "I will not die until the queen
returns to her throne." Here is the response of her younger sister,
a true annexationist: "Both she and I will die before that because
the queen will never return to the throne." I truly believe that
the reaction of the younger sister is the correct one. I myself will
throw the chiefs out of their positions.]

Nā Kia'i o ke Ao were staunch proannexationists. In fact, in a follow-up article, they state, "O ka hoohui aku ia kakou me Amerika, o ia ka hana kupono
nou, e Hawaii, e hana ai [Joining together with America is the right thing
for you to do, O Hawai'i]."[41] Their position therefore influenced the way they
interpreted Kapihe's words. While both articles agree that Kapihe's prophecy was fulfilled with the overthrow of the queen in 1893, they disagree on
whether or not this was a positive or negative event for the people. Thus,
in the months preceding the illegal annexation of Hawai'i, this small debate was but one example of many that filled the newspapers, and whether
the writers were standing as "aloha 'āina," as patriots, or as "ho'uhui 'āina,"
or proannexationists, the fact remains that each voice contributed to larger
discussions on nationhood, resistance, and sovereignty, all of which have
influenced contemporary discourse.

Kahiki as Sanctuary

What these texts provide us with is an invitation to dig into the many possible
meanings of the wānana and to use them in our own ways. As Kauako'iawe
states, "He olelo nane ka Kapihe [Kapihe's prophecy is a riddle]."[42] While
possibly speaking to the ambiguity of Kapihe's words, he could also be suggesting that rather than reading the wānana as a literal account, it would be
more valuable to search for the hidden meaning in the text, and, perhaps,
to even use it to speak to our lives as we live them. Kauako'iawe, Nā Kia'i o
ka Pō, and Nā Kia'i o ke Ao certainly did so, not following those who came
before them but adding to the genealogy of ideas birthed from this prophecy.
They analyzed the words of Kapihe and used them to make sense of their
lives and what they were experiencing in Hawai'i in the mid- to late 1800s.
Their words, as Epeli Hau'ofa explains, are indicative of "what we have been
doing all along," which is "constructing our pasts, our histories, from vast

storehouses of narratives, both written and oral, to push particular agendas."[43] Thus, peering into their articles is important because, although some of them may not push the resistant, anti-American agenda that many who chant Kapihe's words today would like to see, they provide evidence that taking a narrative from the past and interpreting it, or reinterpreting it to make a point, is nothing new.

In writing this book, therefore, I will take inspiration from Kapihe and argue that there is opportunity to not only continue using contemporary versions of his prophecy—like the one being chanted at Puʻuhonua o Puʻuhuluhulu—but to also call upon older renditions, using them to speak to our lives and engagements today. Kahiki, I believe, is the space to do so. As expressed in the introduction to this book, Kahiki, for me, is a sanctuary. It is a place for contemplation, a place for confronting difficult truths, and a place for readying oneself to engage with the world differently. In studying the prophecy of Kapihe, I have learned that Kahiki is also a place for imagining alternative futures. This kind of space, as Harjo explains, is where we can "dream, imagine, speculate, and activate the wishes of our ancestors, contemporary kin, and future relatives—all in a present temporality, which is Indigenous futurity."[44] In considering her words, however, I don't think that we can (or should want to) activate the wishes of *all* of our ancestors but rather those of the ancestors whose desires match our own. We cannot, if we are truly going to honor historical agency, conflate their hopes and dreams, referring to them as a unified group and assuming that they were all on the same page. In my own genealogy, for example, I descend from people who protested annexation, signing the antiannexation Kūʻē Petitions, and people who advocated for it.[45] Therefore, in recognizing their desires, I must choose selectively, respecting their choices in the contexts in which they lived while also using hindsight to my advantage to find those imaginings that can connect to the future I am trying to build today. That is radical sovereignty, and that is an exercise of agency that my descendants will be able to look upon as an example of how I sought to use the past strategically to motivate my present in preparation for a future I cannot yet know but can continuously hope for.

In my personal space for sustained imagining, I'd like to propose that we perhaps look beyond just "Indigenous futurities" that "seek to transform settler colonialisms for all who are caught within such relations of violence and exclusion."[46] In reflecting on the problematics of the term "Indigenous," particularly in Oceania, which were teased out in the previous chapter, I believe we should also embrace "Pacific futurities" (emphasizing that we have more than one). Using the version of Kapihe's prophecy recorded by Kauakoʻiawe, I'd like to suggest that we seek ways to unify Kahiki and Hawaiʻi, Kahiki being the knowledge that we connect to the Pacific region and the act of considering, critiquing, and strengthening our relationships. I do not believe that we have to suspend our loyalties to individual island groups or nations to do so. In fact, when Hauʻofa advocated for a regional Oceania identity, he did not call for abandoning national identities, reiterating instead that they could supplement and support one another.[47] Thus, while I can chant Kapihe's prophecy for Mauna Kea—calling for reversal and envisioning a future in which my descendants will no longer have to struggle to protect it—I can also revive other versions of his words, using them in different contexts that stretch beyond Hawaiʻi's shores.

Perhaps a chant I can give sound and voice to today is, as Kauakoʻiawe records, "E iho mai ana ke akua e noho pu me kanaka, a e pii aku ana hoi ko lalo nei i luna, a e hui ana hoi na pae moku mai Kahiki a Hawaii nei i hookahi [God will descend to dwell with the people, and those here below will ascend, and the archipelagos, from Kahiki to Hawaiʻi, will be united as one]."[48] The "God" of this chant can be open to interpretation, not necessarily representing the Christian god while at the same time not necessarily denying it. It can be a call for Pacific peoples to rise to meet the challenges that they/we face, whether as individual island groups or as a region, and to know that they/we will have support from relatives in Oceania. As a prophecy it can speak to the past, the present, and the future, always adapting to the times and changing circumstances. More importantly, however, it can serve as constant encouragement to not wait for the future to come, but to create it now. As a friend of mine, Bryan Kamaoli Kuwada, once wrote, "We live in the future. Come join us."[49] That is futurity.

In closing this chapter, I will draw inspiration from Hōkūlani Aikau, finding comfort and safety in Kahiki to dream Pacific futurities. In her essay "Following the Alaloa Kīpapa of our Ancestors: A Trans-Indigenous Futurity without the State (United States or Otherwise)," she concludes with an invitation to join her in "envisioning new conditions of possibility," and to "follow the alaloa kīpapa [a long path paved with stones] that leads toward alternative preferred futures that do not require the nation-state as the only legitimate and intelligible governing entity for the enactment of peoples' sovereignty."[50] Considering the diversity of colonial realities in the Pacific—some of us settler colonies, some of us former colonies with sustained relationships with colonial powers, and some of us independent—we cannot limit our futures to only those that are free from the nation-state. Pacific futurities should include those but should also encompass so much more. My invitation, rather, is for us to envision Pacific futurities that do not include us being divided by imposed boundaries, whether those marking the three subregions of the Pacific—Polynesia, Melanesia, and Micronesia—or those "marking" some of us as "Indigenous" (or dispossessed and displaced minorities in our homelands) and some of us not. My invitation is for us to envision Pacific futurities that do not stop at language differences, finding ways to bring the Anglophone, Francophone, Hispanophone, and Sinophone

Pacifics together. The latter is especially critical if we are going to cease seeing Taiwan as the ultimate and almost mythical Pacific homeland, the ultimate Kahiki, and start engaging with its peoples in more meaningful ways. My invitation is to look beyond each other's issues and to do the work to see past and through the dominant frames and references that we've been attached to. It is to understand West Papua as more than genocide, Tuvalu as more than climate change, Nauru as more than phosphate mining, Vanuatu and the Solomon Islands as more than blackbirding, Rapa Nui as more than deforestation, the Marshall Islands as more than nuclear testing and waste, Niue as more than emigration to New Zealand, Guåhan (Guam) as more than US military expansion, Tahiti as more than Gauguin's paintings, Tonga as more than its obesity rates, Fiji as more than political coups, Papua New Guinea as more than cannibalism, the Cook Islands as more than a captain's name, and Hawai'i as more than cultural loss. It is an invitation to look to how our own epistemologies and ontologies, unique to place, can serve as opportunities to connect in (k)new ways. It is an invitation, for instance, to Hawaiians to use Kahiki as a means of remembering our genealogical ties to the Pacific so that we can know it like we know our own families, intimately, and acknowledging the ways we connect and the multitude of ways we are different. It is an invitation to think about what some of our ancestors may have wanted for the region and to know that we already have everything we need to carry their desires through, creating the conditions of possibility with which our descendants can live in a future that, although seemingly radical today, will be better for the region and the world. Join me in Kahiki so that we can dream together.

4

EVERYTHING ANCIENT
WAS ONCE NEW

Kahiki and Persistence

I remember being woken up by the sound of my phone inundated with messages, texts coming from home, telling me to look at the news: in the dark early morning of June 20, 2019, a hale (house) and two ahu (altars) were desecrated on Mauna Kea. In what kiaʻi Kahoʻokahi Kanuha describes as something akin to a "drug raid," law enforcement went to the mauna at three o'clock, before the sun could rise and the day could bear witness, and dismantled our structures.[1] Kanuha was arrested for trying to document their unjust actions. I remember squinting into the glow of my phone, steadying my eyes on the screen, to see photos of Hale Kūkiaʻimauna, a thatched house built across the road from the Mauna Kea visitor's center, in pieces. My mind and heart immediately went to my friend Tee Henderson and her sister, Kara Henderson, two women who led the construction of the hale, simultaneously providing a space and a symbol for a growing movement while also challenging the notion that this type of work is for men alone. The hale was built in two days, beginning on April 12, 2015, during a sustained effort to protect Mauna Kea from the construction of the controversial, and incredibly damaging, Thirty Meter Telescope (TMT), a fight that continues as I write this.

Upon its completion, the hale became a place for kiaʻi, or protectors, in both physical and spiritual form. It was a structure that grew out of the movement and that carried all of our hopes, commitments, and actions toward protecting the mauna and our futures with it. When the hale was dismantled, the state attorney general Clare Connors reported that it, along with the two ahu built at the proposed site of the TMT, "had no traditional or customary significance."[2] I read the news and cried. (In fact, the weight of that memory still makes me cry.) "Why are we not allowed to age?" I thought. "Why are our structures, created in this moment in time, not allowed to grow old?" As I started the day, across the ocean, in Aotearoa, I carried the weight of one phrase with me: "Everything ancient was once new." These words sat on my shoulders, sinking into my chest, until I let them out in a poem, the poem that starts this book and the poem from which this book has taken its name. In the lines that poured out of my grief, I tried to remind people of a simple truism: everything created starts as new, and significance deepens when the "new" is given time to age. My poem, therefore, was a call for time: time to grow, time to evolve, time to change, and time to *be* in the *now* for the future.

When the structures were taken down, Kanuha called the desecration an act of "cultural erasure."[3] He was right. What I felt that morning, though, and what still tugs at my gut, is the fact that this particular type of erasure is one that seeks to control the ways that we are allowed to exist in the world. The attorney general's statement about "traditional and customary significance" was really a statement about age. Because the hale and ahu were not "ancient," they were not important. In the eyes of the settler state, they were not sacred. They were not deserving of protection, care, or even respect. Thus, the logic of erasure employed was one that essentially denies our right to exist as Indigenous peoples in the current time. What is terribly destructive about this is that it both relegates us as Kānaka Maoli to a state of perpetual infancy, in which we are never allowed to move beyond "newness," while also constructing time as the primary measuring stick for "authenticity." If time could be used as proof that the hale and ahu were not "authentic" or "traditional," having not been built precontact (or even postcontact, but with sufficient time to deem them "old enough"), then our claims to them— whether political, cultural, or spiritual—could be disregarded as irrelevant.[4] In the process, *we* could be disregarded as irrelevant.

Accusations of "newness" meant to discredit us, or shackle us to static notions of Indigeneity, are nothing new. In fact, during the Hawaiian Renaissance, a movement beginning in the late 1960s and early 1970s— characterized by George Kanahele as "a rebirth of artistic and intellectual achievement accompanied by a revival of interest in the past, and an increasing pursuit of knowledge and learning"—Kānaka Maoli were sometimes charged with being "inauthentic" as a result of our actions and creations being both not "ancient" and not "pure" or untainted by modernity.[5] The

renaissance, coinciding with what is often called either the Hawaiian movement or the Hawaiian sovereignty movement, bolstered a reactivated and
reinvigorated commitment to ea, or the life and sovereignty of our lands,
waters, and people. In such a rich time of renewed activism and creative and
intellectual growth, it is not surprising that the settler state—or those ben-
efitting from our suppression—would find ways to discredit Kānaka. What
was (and is) distressing, however, is the fact that Kānaka Maoli themselves/
ourselves sometimes adopted these policing measures, judging others for
authenticity. Perhaps even more problematically, as will be explained in this
chapter, is that we sometimes kept ourselves from growing and aging. Years
ago, I found these issues strikingly visible in the canoe renaissance, a subject
that will be explored in the pages ahead.

While conducting research for my PhD, the work that serves as the
basis of this book, I collected oral histories from a group of kālai waʻa, or
canoe builders, who built *Mauloa*, a twenty-six foot outrigger waʻa (canoe),
entirely out of natural materials in the early 1990s. Their mission then, rid-
ing the momentum of the Hawaiian Renaissance and the revitalization of
noninstrument navigation and wayfinding in Hawaiʻi, was to revive the art
of canoe building, including all of the ceremonies and protocols associated
with it. One afternoon, about a year into my PhD journey, I sat with some of
them, listening to their spoken memories, their canoe sitting just beside us
needing repairs and maintenance. I watched some of them weep and heard
the urgency in their voices: their stories needed to be recorded, told, heard,
and, perhaps most importantly, used to help us understand ourselves, how
far we've come as people, and where we want to go. Their story, like that of
my friend Tee and her sister Kara, who built Hale Kūkiaʻimauna, was one of
constructing in the now for the future. It was an act, as the previous chapter
discussed, of Indigenous futurity. After conducting those interviews, however, and even featuring them prominently in my completed PhD thesis,
I've started to think about them differently, particularly in the context of
the current movement to protect Mauna Kea and the dismantling of our
structures on it.

Before I progress, I should note that the history of *Mauloa* is intimately
tied to the mauna. The stones used to make the adze that were fashioned
to carve the canoe, for example, came from a quarry on the mountain. The
canoe builders also generally agree that the life of any canoe begins in the
uplands, where the materials necessary to build it come from. Thus, today,
some of the same men who built *Mauloa* have been, and continue to be,
kiaʻi for Mauna Kea. With that said, I do not want to imply that opposition to the TMT is universal among those who were involved in the revival
of navigation and wayfinding in Hawaiʻi. One outspoken proponent of the
project, Kalepa Baybayan, is a Kanaka Maoli navigator who has been frank
not only in his support of the telescope but also in his condemnation of the

kiaʻi. In response to a proposed sixty-day moratorium on construction, he "slammed" the proposal and likened the actions of the kiaʻi to that of an "immature adolescent."[6] What is significant about his statement, and heartbreaking as well, is that his words shackle Kānaka to the same perpetual infancy that the attorney general's comments and the dismantling of our structures did. In his statements, therefore, he too is complicit in prohibiting us (including himself) from growth, thereby denying us age.

In this chapter, I will work with some of these heavy ideas and tensions by using stories from the kālai waʻa. Recounting their journey to build *Mauloa*, for example, I will discuss some of the complexities and binds in cultural revitalization and Indigenous persistence. I've chosen the story of *Mauloa* in particular because of the unique ways it interacts with Kahiki, the centering focus of this book. Unlike larger, double-hulled canoes built before it, such as the famed *Hōkūleʻa*, *Mauloa* never has (and never will) sail beyond Hawaiʻi's shores. Thus, it intrigues me for the more symbolic ways it connects to Kahiki, or lands beyond, and the opportunity it provides to comment on issues of authenticity, "tradition," and revival. In addition to confronting some of the problematics of recontextualization, an integral part of cultural maintenance and survival, I hope to use the story of *Mauloa* to reflect on cultural constructions in the present, seeing how the building of Hale Kūkiaʻimauna and the ahu, for example, both converge with this earlier effort and diverge from it in profound ways.[7] As this chapter focuses on creating culture and the ability (and the right) to age, Kahiki will be framed as a sanctuary, or a space in which we find the freedom—without needing approval from the state or any colonial power—to continue doing and being in the now, and further, where we can combat any challenges to our authenticity.

Building a Canoe

Since the 1970s and the launching of the double-hulled sailing canoe *Hōkūleʻa*, the canoe itself has become a symbol of Hawaiian resurgence, pride, and cultural identity. In his extensive work in both leading and documenting this profound movement, Ben Finney explains that what initially began as an experiment to prove the intentional rather than accidental settlement of the Pacific by seafaring islanders quickly turned into a cultural phenomenon.[8] The canoe, and *Hōkūleʻa* in particular, became, as Finney describes, "a Hawaiian icon, an attention-grabbing symbol of past glories and future hopes that brought tears to the eyes."[9] Since then, it has continued to influence Kānaka Maoli and other islanders in the Pacific, especially in parts of Polynesia. Part of the reason for this is the fact that the waʻa represents "continuities of identity . . . conjoining past, and present."[10] Thus, it has become a common image and metaphor, often used to evoke feelings of cultural pride, identity, and togetherness; to combat notions of cultural weakness; to stand in opposition to past representations; and to motivate and inspire islanders to view their worlds as wide and expansive rather than small and limited.[11] Additionally, it has served as a physical and tangible reminder of our connections to Kahiki and of our ability to travel over oceans, finding our ways back to each other as Pacific peoples.

Prior to Hōkūleʻa's well-recorded maiden voyage to Tahiti in 1976, crewmembers needed to find someone with the skill to navigate their canoe, as that knowledge had since been forgotten (or at least fell out of practice) in Hawaiʻi.[12] This required them, quite literally, to go to Kahiki, or to lands beyond our shores. Fortunately, Pius Mau Piailug, a navigator from Satawal in the Caroline Islands of Micronesia, came to Hawaiʻi to guide Hōkūleʻa on its voyage to Tahiti. In the process of learning to sail to distant lands, however, some of the crewmembers realized that they had missed a step. In order to sail, you need a canoe. However, what was then deemed another "forgotten" skill was the ability to construct one as their ancestors might have done before Western contact. As Milton "Shorty" Bertelmann (Uncle Shorty[13]), a crewmember on the 1976 voyage, remembers, "Everybody was so awed with the 1976 voyage. But there's so much more . . . . That was just like an event for that one time. But from there . . . it excites all these other dimensions . . . . When we got to Tahiti, everybody went up to Hōkūleʻa and expected to see a koa[14] canoe . . . . But it wasn't. So right there, it's like, ʻOh, maybe we should make one . . .ʼ But [Mau] could see right off the bat that we were disconnected, and not only us there at the canoe, everybody."[15] For Uncle Shorty, the waʻa was his vehicle to "renewal" and to connection or reconnection to a culture he felt separate from. As one of the original crew members of Hōkūleʻa, and one of the first students of Mau Piailug, affectionately called "Papa Mau," Uncle Shorty was in the thick of the renaissance and, more specifically, the growing interest and enthusiasm for canoes. Much of his lifetime, as he explains, had been spent "yearning to go back to the past" and shedding the introduced idea that the past was something to "move aside" or abandon.[16] The canoe, for him, made the past "real," something that he could experience rather than just read about, something that he could embrace rather than run from. Therefore, the logical process of reconnection for him was to bring the past to the present by learning to build canoes, thereby rebuilding (or "remaking"[17]) himself in the process.

After Papa Mau helped guide Hōkūleʻa to Tahiti—and later taught a few select students themselves to navigate and sail on later voyages—Uncle Shorty and a group of other men once again sought the advice, guidance, and instruction of their teacher, asking Papa Mau to be their kahuna kālai waʻa, or the one to lead them in building their canoe. To them, he was "like a living ancestor," or someone who could effectively guide them to the past, using the canoe and its power of continuity to take them on a true voyage of rediscovery to the future.[18] Together with fellow navigator Nainoa Thompson, who Uncle Shorty credits with being the "dreamer" and visionary for the project; his brother and canoe captain, Clayton Bertelmann; and a group of other dedicated Hawaiian men, they embarked on a voyage to build a waʻa using natural materials. What initially began as a dream to build a double-hulled canoe, however, was eventually downsized when it was realized that the natural environment had been so drastically altered that koa trees large enough to build a double-hulled, long-distance sailing vessel were not easy to find. Therefore, the plans were adjusted and the result of this dream was *Mauloa*, the single-hulled, outrigger canoe built and launched in 1992 at Hōnaunau, Kona, on the Big Island of Hawaiʻi.

When I sat down with Uncle Shorty, just over twenty years later, he seemed eager to comment more on the renaissance and on its place in the future than he did on *Mauloa* itself. Upon reflection, I realize that this was quite characteristic of him: always thinking forward, already living in the future, not bound by (or to) time. As I sat with him, then, it quickly became evident that the waʻa, rather than being the main subject of our conversation, would become the vehicle upon which he and I would explore certain concepts together. As we talked, we exchanged memories, reconstructing the past and adding to it.[19] He asked me questions, even probing me to share my hopes for *Mauloa*, not allowing the interview to be a one-way sharing of stories but rather an opportunity to construct them together. In the writing of this chapter, I've taken inspiration from Uncle Shorty. Though I would love to fill these pages with every single memory shared with me—recounting each individual canoe builder's personal rendition of everything from the search for the perfect tree to the ceremonies conducted in the cold of the forest to chopping the trunk and feeling the chips cut their skin to carving the hulls to making ʻaha (sennit rope) on their thighs to lashing pieces together and eventually to launching their canoe—that would be beyond the scope of this individual book. Therefore, I will instead use some of their stories to speak to the issues being addressed in this chapter, hoping that these reflections might contribute to our evolving understanding of cultural revival, particularly as we are continually confronted with accusations of inauthenticity and denied the ability to grow and change.

Reviving and Growing Old

Driving the mission to build *Mauloa* was a sense of cultural loss, or of no longer having the knowledge and skill to do something that our ancestors once did. When people are faced with cultural loss, as Jonathan Lear explains, they have three choices: they can keep performing rituals or customs even though the context in which they were originally practiced no longer exists (and those of the current generation may no longer know what they were initially intended for); they can invent new purposes for the rituals or customs, giving them new meaning and relevance in contemporary times; or they can give the rituals and customs up all together.[20] In the context of *Mauloa*, however, the kālai waʻa did not have a practice to give up; they needed to first revive one and then find ways to give it new relevance by effectively recontextualizing it. In other words, if canoes built from natural materials were no longer part of daily life (thus meaning that the contexts necessitating the skill and knowledge to build them no longer existed), then the practice of kālai waʻa had to be given new functions. Otherwise, the resulting canoe would risk being like other "nostalgic gestures," evoking strong feelings for a romanticized past with little relevance in the present.[21]

As Uncle Shorty remembers, when they approached Papa Mau to help them build a canoe, he thought they were "crazy." In other words, he thought they were so far disconnected and influenced by Western culture that they themselves were "lost." Therefore, before building, as he recalls, Papa Mau said, "Before you build one canoe, you have to make the home."[22] However, when faced with deadlines connected to federal funding, the canoe was built first, without a permanent home secured. In a literal sense, therefore, the waʻa did not have a physical place to be housed, leaving it, as Uncle Shorty remembers, "stranded." Papa Mau's advice to have a permanent house to keep the canoe, however, has meaning far beyond the literal. By "home," I believe he may have also been telling the men to ensure the canoe had a place in society, in the culture, and, in short, in the present. When a practice is revived, in other words, it has to be recontextualized to fit modern lifestyles, and it must be sustainable. Without a place, or without being incorporated into the daily lives of modern Kānaka, in other words, not only the canoe itself but the entire practice of canoe building as well may end up "stranded."

Uncle Shorty's brief discussion of the "home" was later echoed in my very last interview with a kālai waʻa, the late Charlie Grace. When the canoe was built, it was used in educational programs, and taken to schools so that children could learn about it, touch it, and see it. However, in the years following its initial launch, it was often left to sit on the shore, and, as Uncle Charlie recalls, simply, "you cannot do that." A canoe must be used. However, to take care of it after it is built is a monumental task, especially for people who do not have the time or the resources to maintain it.[23] "Everybody wants a canoe," he states. "The canoe looks good. But to take care of the canoe, nobody was doing [it]."[24] He told me that many of the canoe builders had to return to their jobs, their families, and their lives once the project was over. Therefore, the maintenance of the canoe became the responsibility of a select few. This proved to be difficult, especially since *Mauloa* had no permanent home, either in the physical world or, in some ways, in the cultural world. *Mauloa* became a moment, a gesture that was then left to sit, its pandanus sails and koa hulls—while holding the profound stories of its creation—eventually falling victim to disuse.

Reflecting on their words, I believe they present a lesson about renaissance and revival, particularly about the need to maintain knowledge and unique ways of knowing as much as we strive to also protect our physical objects or structures. As Michael Chandler argues, "If any fulsome sense of indigenous identity is to be maintained, it will need to rest its case more upon the *processes* than on the fraying *contents* of culture—more upon identifying and inhabiting indigenous ways of knowing and meaning making than upon any more transient efforts to archive even a whole museum of increasingly antique cultural shards."[25] In other words, when we protect something so intently, turning it into a relic rather than using it as it was intended to be used, do we risk losing the knowledge that comes with its use, repair, and reconstruction? If we do not have to engage, continuously, in the *processes* of building, for instance, will we be left with a canoe that we cannot replicate?

I ask these difficult questions cognizant of the fact that I myself am not a canoe builder or a sailor, first, because canoe building (at least in the case of *Mauloa*) was a job assigned to men, and second, because I lack the skills necessary to be an effective crew member. I therefore pose my questions with the deepest respect for those who shared their memories with me, those who *did* build a canoe and who *do* sail across oceans. As a writer, I've always been committed to telling stories and to seeing how they might help us do what our kūpuna before us have always done: use them to continually explain ourselves to ourselves. Over the years, my engagements with Kahiki, which, as a concept, has always been shifted and adjusted to meet the needs of the time and to explain changing circumstances, have taught me this: stories retold and concepts reused help us to make sense of our lives. The stories of the kālai waʻa have taken on new meaning for me because I've changed and grown *with* them and *because* of them, and also because the world we live in today is different from that of twenty-seven years ago, when *Mauloa* was being built, or even six years ago, when I collected interviews with the canoe builders. Thus, my aim here is to honor their stories by bringing them into the *now* to see how they can speak to—and provide a basis for understanding—some of the complex issues we face today, including that of perpetual infancy mentioned earlier.

What intrigues me about *Mauloa* in the context of the story that opened this chapter, regarding the dismantling and desecration of the hale and ahu on Mauna Kea, is that while I mourned the fact that our structures were denied the opportunity to grow old, I must also ask myself if everything must, or even should, grow old. In other words, must everything "new" become ancient? This question is especially pertinent to *Mauloa*. As an outrigger canoe, one capable of being sailed in coastal areas, and perhaps used as a small fishing vessel, it is interesting to reflect on the fact that what once would have given *Mauloa* function and import is now what it is being protected from—wear and tear as a functional vessel—so that it can age and be preserved for some future time. If this is the primary function that the kālai waʻa have given *Mauloa*, to serve as a cultural symbol rather than a functional canoe, then what can be said of our futurity? As explored in the previous chapter, if our Indigenous futurity as Kānaka Maoli is about operating in the now "in service to our ancestors, contemporary relatives and future relatives," we would be remiss not to consider how *Mauloa* will be of service to our future generations.[26] Canoes built of natural materials that function as such are perhaps not meant to be ancient. Perhaps they are meant to be used, meant to be worn, meant to be repaired, and meant to eventually be retired, and then returned to the earth. *Mauloa*, however, as a canoe that is not used as one, has become the symbol of a story, of a movement, and of the renaissance in general. Therefore, what must be considered in telling its stories and relaying them to future listeners/readers is what is both lost and gained in the choices we make about how to use what we create and construct. *Not* using *Mauloa* as a canoe, while requiring the kālai waʻa to learn and master the skills necessary for upkeep, maintenance, and restoration that comes with time, may inadvertently cause them to miss out on the opportunity to master *Mauloa* in the water, guiding the canoe's heavy hulls through currents and waves. In other words, if we have a waʻa, as Chandler reminds us, but do not sail it, do we risk losing the ways of knowing and doing that come with sailing these types of vessels?[27] In short, are we left with a symbol of our resurgence and the possibility of needing a subsequent revival?

When Hale Kūkiaʻimauna was constructed on Mauna Kea, it was both symbolic and functional. It represented the movement, or the coming together of kiaʻi to protect our mauna, while also serving as a space where they could gather, sing, pray, teach, and even plan and strategize. Thus, my sadness the morning it was destroyed was not because it wouldn't be able to become a static relic of culture—especially since the natural materials it was built with would have prohibited that and required repair and upkeep—but because our children and future generations were robbed of the chance to learn about hale in one that had been built for them. The hale had been constructed with them in mind, with every intention to provide them with both a symbol of our commitment to standing for their futures and the shelter for them to continue to do so for their own descendants. The key difference between *Mauloa* and the hale, therefore, is that one was destroyed because of how it functioned and the ways its very functionality serviced our Indigenous futurities. In other words, it was destroyed because it challenged attempts to keep us in perpetual childhood, unable to age and grow with and for our future relatives. The other endures—at least as far as the settler state is concerned—because its function is not threatening. As long as it stands as a symbol of the past, in other words, it cannot disrupt visions of a non-Indigenous future, or settler futurities.

The destruction of the hale and ahu on Mauna Kea sent a clear message to Kānaka Maoli: our very existence as contemporary beings is what renders us, and our cultural creations, illegitimate. In the eyes of the settler state, in other words, to be Kānaka Maoli we either have to be dead (and therefore part of a precontact, pure past) or only just Hawaiian enough to not threaten the colonial power. Noelani Goodyear-Kaʻōpua has previously written about what she calls "settler safety zones," or zones that are state-sanctioned areas designated for cultural practice where "just enough 'culture' is allowable, so long as it does not threaten or undermine settler-colonial relations of power."[28] Extending her argument, however, I would also argue that our bodies, policed and often criminalized (as seen in Kanuha's arrest mentioned earlier), are given sanctions to be and do certain things deemed just cultural enough to give the state its distinctiveness and allow it to continue to sell Hawaiʻi as a premiere tourist destination. After his arrest for trying to halt the desecration of our structures on Mauna Kea, Kanuha was interviewed. He said:

What the state of Hawaiʻi has showed again is that, in their mind, Hawaiians, me, Kahoʻokahi Kanuha, I'm a fake person. I'm a fake Hawaiian. My dad is a fake Hawaiian. My brother is a fake Hawaiian. My grandpa is a fake Hawaiian. Everybody who stands up there on Mauna Kea, they're all fake Hawaiians. All the cops that arrest us, those Hawaiians, fake Hawaiians. None of us, none of us are real because there are other ahu on that mauna. There are other structures; there's lele [altars or stands for offerings]. But they were built, perhaps, longer ago. There are other structures in Hawaiʻi that would never be touched because they were built 200 years ago, they were built 300 years ago, they was built 500 years ago.[29] Those things need to protect, but anything that was built in modern history, by a modern, current living Hawaiian, that's all for show. That's only good on the stage, with the ʻukulele and the plumeria lei, with Hawaiian Airlines in the background. That's all it's good for. Hawaiian is only good for the government and the state of Hawaiʻi, their agencies, making all these make-believe, fake hula shows, Polynesian lūʻaus . . . that's "Hawaiian," that we're proud of, that we can have. But, if you, you fake Hawaiian, try to be real, and you try to go up to the mauna and protect something that you built, just like your kūpuna built, well that, we don't have time for that.[30]

In his explanation, Kanuha highlights what some call a "double bind of Indigeneity," or an impossible situation in which "the more modern or global indigeneity is seen as being, the more its authenticity as an identity is questioned."[31] In other words, as mentioned previously, our modernity makes us somehow less-than real as Indigenous peoples. It is precisely because we exist in the *now* and have been shaped (at least in part) by modern influences and globalization, in other words, that we are seen as incapable of producing anything "real."

As Kanuha demonstrated, once our physical bodies become too much, or once we question our relegation to the realm of "fake," stretching beyond what the state has "allowed" us to be, we are reprimanded. Our presence on the mountain, for example, is a challenge to colonial structures of power, and our hale and ahu are visible representations of our presence and of our ongoing commitment to challenging those structures into the future. This is the double bind, or one of the "catch-22s of indigeneity": exist within the settler-determined confines of Indigeneity without punishment or break out of those confines and be reprimanded.[32] In the first instance, you risk "playing" Hawaiian, and in the second you risk being Hawaiian while constantly having to prove yourself against settler definitions of who and what we can and should be.

When we relate the hale and the ahu to *Mauloa*, however, we see a different kind of "double bind," perhaps one that works in even more insidious ways. Our presence in a canoe, while still a political act and while still important, has come to be accepted, and in some cases, even co-opted, by the state as another point of distinction and difference. The canoe is so accepted, in fact, that it has become somewhat emblematic of Hawaiʻi. In her reflections on writing about culture, Kirin Narayan argues that "'natives' tied to particular places are also associated with particular *ideas*."[33] In other words, when so much writing and research is dedicated to certain concepts or cultural phenomena, examining them becomes normalized. It becomes as natural, for example, to study the canoe and cultural renaissance in Hawaiʻi and in Polynesia as it has become to go "to India to study worship, the circum-Mediterranean region for honor and shame, China for ancestor worship, and so on, forgetting that anthropological preoccupations represent 'the temporary *localization* of ideas from *many* places.'"[34] The bind here, therefore, is that while all of the research and writing about waʻa in Hawaiʻi is generative, empowering, and useful, it can also begin to lock us into particular framings, shaping what is and isn't acceptable in society. In saying this, I must implicate myself as someone who continues to be fascinated by, and deeply engaged in, studying the canoe renaissance. Thus, while my writing both seeks to highlight specific stories, such as those about *Mauloa*, it also contributes to the growing expectation that this is something Kānaka Maoli will study and write about. The canoe, in other words, is becoming as emblematic of Hawaiʻi as hula and surfing. Since these are all incredibly rich, deep, and complex topics, inspiring years of research past, present, and future, how do we continue to write about them in ways that do not sustain the settler state's sanctioning of them? While I certainly do not have a quick response or solution, I believe that examining the link between *Mauloa* and Kahiki may provide us with ways to think through these binds.

Kahiki in a Single-Hulled Canoe

Kahiki, as the life-giving and life-sustaining homeland from which our first ancestors came, is our genealogical link to the rest of the Pacific. However, as explored in previous chapters, what was once a term used to explain origins in Oceania, as seen in oral traditions, eventually became a term used to refer to all lands outside of Hawaiʻi. As such, Kahiki could be found in everything from the stories of great migrating ancestors to nineteenth-century newspaper texts pushing nationalistic sentiments, or sometimes even justifying support for annexation, topics discussed in chapter 3. Tracking the complex and often messy genealogy of this concept, while allowing us to peer into the minds of those who used it, also gives us permission to do the same. When the kālai waʻa built *Mauloa*, they may not have used "Kahiki" as a specific term in their interviews with me. However, I would argue that they acted upon their Kahiki connections—or the knowledge of being genealogically linked to other parts of the Pacific—to combat accusations of inauthenticity. When Papa Mau returned to Hawaiʻi from Satawal to help the men, he came to teach them how to use their own resources, or materials that could be sourced in Hawaiʻi, to build their canoe. Since the dominant message at the time was that the kālai waʻa were endeavoring to build an "authentic" or "traditional" canoe—words that many of them still use in their stories today— their decision to bring in Papa Mau was both celebrated and criticized.[35]

While some applauded their efforts, others made remarks about the resulting canoe, saying that it was not "Hawaiian" but "Micronesian." (I should note here that calling *Mauloa* a "Micronesian" canoe is quite problematic in that it assumes that all islands in the region known as Micronesia—composed of more than two thousand islands and atolls—built/build canoes in the same way.) As Uncle Charlie remembers, "People started looking at the canoe and a lot of people started questioning: this no look like Hawaiian canoe.[36] . . . But when the project was given, they told Mau, 'Make canoe.' He said, 'Okay.' But nobody told him the design of the canoe. So Mau wen just design the canoe like his home."[37] When I sat down with some of the men twenty years after they built their canoe, many of them seemed to find ways to defend their work against criticism, even by fellow Kānaka. One kālai waʻa, Angel Pilago, spoke about how entering a space of learning with Papa Mau required him to make personal sacrifices, including changing his behavior and attitude in order to work for what he called "inclusiveness," or a way of bringing identities together. He explains:

> We have to be willing to sacrifice parts of ourselves to build composites of who and what we are . . . . *Mauloa* is a composite, a composite of Micronesian from the West, Marquesan in the East [one of the lead carvers, named Tava Taupu, was from the Marquesas], and Hawaiians in the middle . . . with all their identities, Pacific identities, there needed to be one canoe that has a universal inclusiveness. That's *Mauloa* . . . . The only person who had the mana [power] to do that was Mau. There's no other person who could do that but him.[38]

According to Uncle Angel, it was precisely because Papa Mau came from Kahiki, or from outside of Hawai'i, that he was able to help the men embrace not only who they were as Kānaka Maoli but who they were as people of the region as well. When he spoke about making sacrifices, he meant that because they did not have a teacher in Hawai'i, he had to confront the fact that they could not get everything they needed to build their canoe at home. Thus, the meaning of "traditional" and "authentic" had to change and stretch to be inclusive of Kahiki. In the process, although the kālai wa'a knew that *Mauloa* would never leave Hawai'i's shores, they spoke of profound journeys, journeys that allowed them to discover the depths of who they were, not just as Indigenous people in Hawai'i but as Oceanic people as well.

Drawing on a connection to Kahiki was not a strategic or convenient move to serve their agenda or to justify their canoe. Rather, it was a return to older ways of thinking that were not so isolated or guarded. One of my worries, in the wake of the Hawaiian Renaissance, has been that the experience of great cultural loss has made us more reserved in our willingness to bring in ideas and tools from the "outside," particularly when dealing with customs and practices deemed "traditional." This has, in some ways, stagnated us, and is one of the reasons "traditional" is such a troubling and limiting word for Indigenous peoples. As Albert Wendt articulates in his often-quoted essay "Towards a New Oceania," "There is no state of cultural purity (or perfect state of cultural *goodness*) from which there is decline: usage determines authenticity."[39] The mere suggestion that something can be, or ever has been, "traditional," in other words, implies that there is only one real way to be, or do, or create. The building of *Mauloa*, therefore, offset this notion of traditionality by effectively bringing in knowledge from Kahiki and proving that culture can be, and is always, made in the *now*. At the same time, however, it also reinforced false notions of authenticity; thus the impossible bind. In the act of becoming a symbol of culture rather than a functional canoe, in other words, it has been captured in time and therefore bolsters the idea of

Indigeneity as living in the past rather than growing up in the present. Using Kahiki as a conceptual tool, however, I believe is useful in helping us to work out of, or at least be aware of, these binds.

Kahiki as Sanctuary

Recorded in a songbook for Queen Emma, the wife of one of Kamehameha's sons, Alexander Liholiho Kamehameha IV, is a mele, or chant, about the building of a canoe. Although it is not entirely clear when the mele was initially composed, it was dedicated to Queen Emma's brother-in-law, Lot Kapuāiwa Kamehameha V, who ruled in the 1860s. Thus in the years Lot governed Hawai'i, or perhaps at some point in the nineteenth century, the mele honors Kahiki, stating,

> 'O ia ka hiki o ka wa'a
> Ō ho'okala i Kahiki ke ko'i kua wa'a
> Kua i kona wa'a kaikaina nui.

> [That is the origin of the canoe
> Do sharpen in Kahiki the canoe carving adze
> Carve out the canoe to be like a great younger sibling.][40]

Although recorded generations earlier—and in just three lines taken out of many—the mele seems to speak to the experiences of the men who built *Mauloa* as if composed during their time. The origin of *Mauloa* was indeed in Kahiki, in a land outside of Hawai'i. It was from there, from a place and a people genealogically older than Kānaka Maoli, that Papa Mau came to Hawai'i to teach them how to make their own adze so that they could shape and carve not only their canoe but also themselves as Hawaiian men.

If we are to find our ways through, or perhaps out of, some of the double binds we are so often caught up in, however, I believe we have to look at Kahiki as more than a place from which to source materials and knowledge. I believe we have to use Kahiki as a sanctuary, or the space where our Indigenous futurities thrive and where settler futurities do not. In other words, Kahiki cannot be the place and space we retreat to when we need to defend ourselves against accusations of inauthenticity. Defending ourselves reinforces the state-imposed expectations and parameters of Indigeneity. Instead, Kahiki must be the place where we use our connections to one another to work against state-sanctioned limits and rules put on Indigenous cultures and bodies. It must be the space where the permission, allowance, and measurements of authenticity do not—and cannot—exist. It is where those things are rendered meaningless. It is where the only "realness" needed is what is being created in the *now* for the future.

When Kanaka Maoli navigator Kalepa Baybayan called kiaʻi on Mauna Kea immature adolescents, he supported a settler futurity, arguing that Hawaiians needed to learn how to share Mauna Kea. In the process, he sought to provide space—both literally and conceptually—for settler desires to both endure and prosper. At the same time, however, his very Indigeneity was used by the governor of Hawaiʻi, David Ige, as a weapon against other Kānaka Maoli. Baybayan is presented as the "good" Hawaiian, as the proof that we can "get along" and share (implying that we can compromise and give up on ourselves and our Indigenous futures). Those of us who refuse to compromise the life and health of our mauna, therefore, are the "bad" children in need of discipline. The desecration of our structures on Mauna Kea, then, was a punishment against those of us who have misbehaved. When viewing this alongside the story of *Mauloa*, we are able to examine the underpinning assumptions about Indigeneity that we may unconsciously live our lives by. Why is *Mauloa* allowed to live while the hale and ahu are not? While I still grieve the loss of our structures, what Kahiki provides us is the freedom to keep creating in the ways that we decide are appropriate *today*. Just as the kālai waʻa were able to bring in knowledge from Kahiki, we can too. However, in learning from that story, we can use Kahiki to strengthen what we do and create *now* so that they have function, relevance, and context to continue to exist into the future. In other words, Kahiki is the conceptual tool that helps us not only work out of impossible binds but, hopefully, get rid of them all together. It is the only permission we need to continue constructing ideas and structures that will both teach and serve as shelters for our future generations.

5

TO THE BONES

Kahiki and "Discovery"

During one of my visits to Ihumātao in 2019, where mana whenua are protecting their land in Auckland, my friend, a fiercely intelligent woman named Tina Ngata, invited me to speak with her on the Doctrine of Discovery and how the assumptions created and maintained by the doctrine continue to manifest today. Sitting under a tent, the chill of the early August evening setting in, we gathered with an intimate crowd to discuss colonial fictions and Indigenous truths. Needless to say, we knew the content would be heavy, even potentially emotional, and that talking about issues of invasion, colonialism, white supremacy, and racism would become even heavier while sitting on the whenua at Ihumātao, where people were camped as a result of these realities. Therefore, we started by going around the circle, each of us introducing ourselves and speaking briefly about why we were there. Knowing each other's names and where we came from helped to turn what could have been a dense lecture into a conversation that, although difficult at times, was (and still is) necessary. The Doctrine of Discovery is not something that usually comes up in every day conversation (even my own). However, as we talked about that evening, we cannot ignore the impact the doctrine has had (and continues to have) on our lives as Indigenous Pacific peoples.

The Doctrine of Discovery, which "might be more accurately called the doctrine of Christian European arrival, or, better still, the doctrine of Christian invasion," allowed for the violent raid and seizure of lands belonging to non-Christians.[1] Vine Deloria explains that the doctrine, issued in the fifteenth century, provided opportunity for Christian nations to "discover" the lands of non-Christians, giving them "legal title regardless of the claims and rights of the existing inhabitants."[2] It was, in other words, "an agreement among thieves" that dehumanized Indigenous peoples as a means of justifying colonialism.[3] That evening, Tina and I wanted to talk about how assumptions premised on the doctrine are still alive and operating today, even manifesting at Ihumātao and Mauna Kea. At the annual meeting of the Native American and Indigenous Studies Association (NAISA) conference earlier in the year, Debra Harry—who was on a panel with Tina and other Indigenous scholars—explained quite pointedly, "These colonial systems of domination are now embedded in the colony, in the law, in the policies, in the minds, in the beliefs. . . . There's still this fundamental belief that Indigenous peoples and other peoples of color are less than human. That has not gone away."[4] As we looked around the camp at Ihumātao, the dark setting in, the cold settling into our bones, I knew that was true.

Our conversation was timely, not only because of the protective actions and movements unfolding in both in Hawai'i and in Aotearoa but also because of the upcoming Tuia—Encounters 250 (Tuia 250), the New Zealand government's planned commemoration for Captain Cook's invasion of Aotearoa 250 years earlier, on October 6, 1769.[5] Although the organizers preferred to use terms like "landing," "arrival," or, as the full name of Tuia 250 indicates, "encounter," these names were nothing but an attempt to mask what Cook's "arrival" in Aotearoa truly was: an invasion justified by the Doctrine of Discovery. While the government and the organizers of the commemorative event used terminology strategically, the realities of racism, violence, and colonialism remained. This is what Tina and I wanted to unravel and expose, providing language and frameworks for understanding and articulating some of the injustices we experience as Indigenous peoples today, particularly in settler colonies like Hawai'i and Aotearoa.

In the lead-up to Tuia 250, I had to take pause to consider my role here in Aotearoa. I am not tangata whenua (Indigenous to this place); I am not Māori. I am also not part of the dominant settler society nor of the large populations of Pacific peoples who migrated here for employment and education beginning in the 1950s and 1960s. I consider myself to be Indigenous but am deeply aware of the fact that I am not living in the place I am Indigenous to. Therefore, I constantly ask myself what my roles and responsibilities are to this place as a Hawaiian woman positioned somewhere between the dominant categories existent here. When I first moved to Aotearoa in 2012, I met a Māori woman (who later became my dear friend) who insisted that I was not a Pacific Islander. Although Hawaiʻi is indeed a Pacific Island, she would not categorize me with those she already knew of as being "Pacific," a category that means very specific things in Aotearoa.[6] To her, I was not Māori; I was not white; I was not an Islander; I was simply Hawaiian. In the years following her insistence that I be categorized differently and on my own, I've had to consider what that positionality means, what responsibilities it leaves me with, and, perhaps even more importantly, what occupying a liminal space can allow me to do or say.

This chapter was born out of my consideration of her once telling me, "You're not an islander; you're Hawaiian." Her words took on particular importance as I started to engage critically with Tuia 250 and thought about what I could contribute to conversations about what the commemoration meant (and continues to mean). Having come to Aotearoa from Hawaiʻi, I am acutely aware of the ongoing impacts of settler colonialism; I recognize them at home, and I recognize them here. Although colonized by different nations, I believe we can see ourselves reflected in each other's experiences, in each other's struggles, and, in many ways, in each other's histories of resistance and survival. If I'm being completely honest, though, I sometimes wonder if the bond between Māori and Hawaiians—a close bond often recognized and commented on by both those within these two communities and not—has been in some ways facilitated by settler colonialism. I wonder, in other words, if our closeness has come from similar experiences of struggle and our ability to recognize the pain that comes with it. When I first started learning about Tuia 250, I was disturbed by it. I recognized settler colonial logics at work in its naming, in its branding, and in the incredibly deceptive rhetoric meant to frame it as something acceptable, even something nationalistic, to "celebrate."

In this chapter I will therefore engage with Tuia 250 as an Indigenous woman, as an arrivant to Aotearoa living on land that is not my own, and as an ally to tangata whenua whose struggles I have a responsibility to help shoulder (in any way that is deemed appropriate). My aim here is to consider what it means to be a Kanaka Maoli in "Kahiki," or on someone else's land in the Pacific, and to acknowledge that my being here comes with certain obligations to the people of this place and to the lands and waters that feed us. In the first chapter of this book, I commented on our ability to embrace both national and regional identities. This chapter is my attempt to act upon that regional identity. To do so, I will analyze Captain Cook as a metaphor for the settler colonial state and reflect upon how and why his death and dismemberment—not just as an event but as a process—matter in this context and in our collective efforts to resist being disrespected, silenced, and erased as Indigenous peoples. In this chapter, Kahiki will be framed as a sanctuary, not necessarily one to find safety and refuge in, but one that forces us to reflect on what it means (or can mean) for Kānaka Maoli to truly participate and cooperate in decolonial movements both here in Aotearoa and, further, in our wider Kahiki. In doing so, I will actually push my genealogical connections to Kahiki to the background, not to ignore them but to ensure that I do not use them to justify my presence in a country that deserves my critical attention. Kahiki will therefore be the motivator for my actions rather than the excuse I use to be too comfortable in a Pacific place that is not my own.[7]

(Un)Settling

At a poetry event at the start of the year, a Māori woman came up to me and asked, "Can I hug you?" She paused briefly and then continued, "I always thought we should have a Hug-a-Hawaiian day to thank you for what you did to Cook." Though some may think her request distasteful considering what we *did* do to Cook, I said, "Sure," before exchanging a warm embrace and a knowing smile. Our short hug was for the fact that on February 14, 1779, captain James Cook was killed in Kealakekua, Hawai'i. While it is not my habit to celebrate the death of anyone, or to exchange hugs in commemoration of their demise, I often find myself in situations like the one described above. As a Hawaiian now living in Aotearoa, I have gotten used to this type of interaction. While I personally had nothing to do with ending Cook's murderous voyages in the Pacific, people in Oceania do remember how and why his life came to an end and sometimes hold my ancestors in high regard for it.

The death of Captain Cook seems all the more meaningful for people (and for some, an appropriate event to celebrate) when seen in the context of Tuia 250, New Zealand's national commemoration recognizing Cook's first invasion at Tūranganui-a-Kiwa (later known as Gisborne) in 1769. It has been reported that more than twenty million dollars was spent on events and resources to "mark" the occasion.[8] Given the fact that this "encounter" had been anything but peaceful and that it resulted in Māori being killed, it should come as no surprise that many protested Tuia 250, rallying support for anti-Cook presentations, demonstrations, and exhibitions.[9] When I first learned about Tuia 250, I was initially a bit hesitant to speak too openly about my opposition to it. I worried that as a non-Māori Kanaka Maoli migrant to Aotearoa I may not be entitled to any opinion, especially while there were Māori who did support it and who did participate. This changed, however, when I thought about what I would want other Pacific peoples (especially those whose ancestors also suffered at the hands of Cook[10]) to do if the roles were reversed and if a 250-year "celebration" were to be held in Hawai'i. I therefore decided to write about it and to present some of my ideas at the NAISA 2019 conference held in Waikato, the same conference where Debra

Harry and Tina Ngata spoke about the Doctrine of Discovery. Cook's invasion in Aotearoa needed to be framed as an invasion, and I realized that my responsibility was to be part of the conversation, bringing what I could from Hawai'i to assist and support the stand against celebrating a voyage of "discovery" that was founded on the assumptions of white supremacy and Indigenous inferiority. To do so, however, I had to get closer to my positionality, to what and who I am in this country, and how that affects the way I present myself and my solidarity.

When I first moved to Aotearoa and settled in Te Whanganui-a-Tara (now known as Wellington), I was adamant about calling myself a "settler." It was a way of keeping myself from ever getting too comfortable here, or from forgetting that my presence in this country was made possible by the settler state. It was a way of never allowing myself to be complicit in the ongoing oppression of tangata whenua. It was not a comfortable identity to embrace, but I felt it was necessary. In using the term, however, I made others uncomfortable. Some of my Māori friends—such as the one referred to earlier—tried to give me alternative labels, more loving labels, reassuring me that, yes, I was different, but that I was not like "them," or like some of the Pākehā (European) who live here oblivious to the fact that they are on Indigenous land *or* who insist that this is "one nation."[11] At the same time, I made Pacific peoples uncomfortable. Like me, they were not Indigenous. However, their histories in Aotearoa were far too complex to be flattened with the label of "settler," as it did not account for historical and colonial relations, such as the fact that Tokelau, the Cook Islands, and Niue are part of the New Zealand realm. My use of the term also brought me into conversation with people who maintained that labels such as "Indigenous" and "settler" are introduced concepts and should therefore be disregarded and abandoned completely.

In considering the feelings and opinions shared with me as I've used the term "settler" to refer to myself, I've had to continually grapple with my place here. While my friend was trying to position me somewhere in the in-between, not native but not completely foreign (due to our genealogical connections across Polynesia and the wider Pacific), but also not part of the "Islander" community in this country, she sought to carve out a unique space for my *being* here. While it would be tempting to find consolation in her well-meaning labeling and, further, in the fact that some Māori hold Hawai'i as a possible place from which their ancestors came, I have not allowed myself to "settle" into positions of comfort. Instead, I prefer to keep myself in check by constantly reflecting on my own experiences growing up as Kanaka Maoli, or an Indigenous person, in Hawai'i's settler colonial society. In other words, I prefer to use my "knowing" of settler colonialism—or my seeing, hearing, and feeling it—to keep me from becoming part of the problem in someone else's homeland.

Knowing what dispossession, displacement, and persistent and intentional disappearance feels like, I see it as my responsibility to be on edge, to be a bit uncomfortable, and to work with and in the tension that my presence creates here in Aotearoa. To *not* do so, I believe, would be to support (even if unconsciously and in indirect and subtle ways) settler colonial projects. I've therefore come to understand how my being Kanaka Maoli can be of use, as it drives my insistence that the settler state never become completely normalized and that *I* never become normalized or complacent with it. Being Hawaiian motivates me to constantly call settler colonialism out, making it visible, even if and when it means implicating myself. Central to my work now is the belief that while "Indigenous" is an introduced concept, when it comes to contexts of settler colonialism, Indigeneity not only matters, it *has to* matter, at least until there is any true decolonization. If we accept, however, Edward Cavanagh's assertion that there is no "clear and inevitable end-point" to settler colonialism and that the goal of settler decolonization is an abstraction at best, then perhaps Indigeneity will always have to matter.[12] My exploration of Tuia 250, my use of Cook as a metaphor for settler colonialism, and my examination of self will hopefully reveal why this is so.

Being Another Other

In order to argue for the place and function of Indigeneity in Aotearoa, it is important to first explain how my initial and strict adherence to the Indigenous/settler binary was problematic and therefore had to shift. It is also critical that I work through a few key terms and concepts that will be instrumental in this chapter. When I was confronted in my use of the term "settler," I was forced to recognize the complexities of different experiences and identities in this country in a way that I was not initially able to as a relatively new migrant. I had to consider, for instance, the important difference between those who came here to settle, erase, and replace and those who were brought here, lured here with promises of opportunity, and then oppressed. Therefore, borrowing from Lorenzo Veracini, I've found it useful to replace my binary thinking with a triangular framework: "The settler colonial situation establishes a system of relationships comprising three different agencies: the settler coloniser, the indigenous colonised, and a variety of differently categorized exogenous 'Others.'"[13] While the category of "exogenous other" is inherently troubling as it does not allow for a full understanding of the diversity *within* that grouping, it is helpful in acknowledging that the there are peoples who must be considered as distinct from the settler colonizer and who have quite often also experienced oppression by the colonial state.

With that said, in this chapter I resist the temptation to categorize and draw distinctions between exogenous others when considering the impacts of settler colonialism because to do so, as Patrick Wolfe explains in his conversation with J. Kēhaulani Kauanui, would be to ignore the fact that no matter our backgrounds or unique experiences, we are all here in Aotearoa because of the settler project. When referring to the "exogenous other" in this way, as Wolfe clarifies,

> that doesn't mean that they haven't suffered, that doesn't mean that they're bad guys. Willingly or not, enslaved or not, at the point of a gun or not, they arrived as part of the settler-colonial project. That doesn't make them settlers in the same sense as the colonizers who coerced them to participate—of course not—but it does make them perforce part of the settler-colonial process of dispossession and elimination. I can't stress strongly enough that it's NOT a matter of volition on their part, and certainly not of culpability. It's just a structural fact.[14]

My being here, for example, *is* a structural fact. I was hired by a university, and as Wolfe said in response to his own positionality as a non-Indigenous person living and working in Australia, "the fact of the matter is that I wouldn't have had a university job if Indigenous people hadn't had their land stolen from them."[15] I live in Te Whanganui-a-Tara, in a city called Wellington, conscious of the fact that this land had to be drastically altered—streams culverted, covered, and disappeared beneath concrete—and people displaced in order for my home and workplace to now be here. I may not have pushed people out myself, but it is important to recognize how I've benefited from their removal.

Borrowing from Caribbean poet Kamau Brathwaite, Jodi Byrd and Judy Rohrer use the term "arrivant" to refer to the "exogenous other" in the triangular framework.[16] Byrd uses the term to refer specifically to people who were forced to "arrive" in the Americas through "the violence of European and Anglo-American colonialism and imperialism around the globe."[17] Rohrer uses it in the context of Hawai'i to refer to those who "arrived" as immigrant laborers to work on the sugar plantations as early as 1852.[18] In Aotearoa, I propose that an arrivant is any non-Indigenous, nonwhite migrant. While acknowledging that this definition is far too general to account for the messiness of the many diverse relationships in this country, I propose it as a tool for sorting through the various positions of people and the positionalities that come with them/us.

In different colonial contexts, whether coming as slaves or as laborers, whether coming in search of (sometimes false) promises of opportunity, at the hand of extreme violence, or in anticipation of education, arrivants had children, created histories, and sometimes—at least in the case of Japanese and Chinese descendants of plantation workers in Hawai'i—eventually adopted the ways of the settler state, assimilated, and rose to economic and political success. Despite their various levels of engagement or disengagement with Indigenous peoples, I've chosen to use the term "arrivant" to refer to all of these migrants as well as their descendants. Although I came here under different circumstances—not forced, not lured, but by my own choice—I now view myself in Aotearoa as an arrivant, or as a non-Indigenous, nonwhite migrant. Doing so allows me to embrace one of Rohrer's goals, which is to flesh out "both histories of leaving and consequences of coming."[19] Whether we physically leave a place and relocate ourselves, or are in a place because of the movement of our ancestors, it is imperative that we think of our arrival—personal or ancestral—and the consequences of our coming to place.

I must make clear, however, that by interrogating the roles of arrivants to Aotearoa, I am not implying that all "exogenous others" experience settler colonialism in the same ways, or that we all had a choice, or an opportunity, to decide how we would benefit (or not) from it. In the context of the United States, Byrd explains, "It is all too easy, in critiques of ongoing U.S. settler colonialism, to accuse diasporic migrants, queers, and people or color for participating in and benefiting from indigenous loss of lands, cultures, and lives and subsequently to position indigenous otherness as abject and all other Others as part of the problem."[20] By examining the consequences of our/my coming, my goal is not to imagine or craft homogenous categories of Indigenous, settler, and arrivant. To do so would be to deny the complexities of experiences, identities, and articulations *within* these groupings and, more problematically, to build upon false notions of an Indigenous authenticity or purity precontact. It would also be to assume that any and all changes postcontact, whether to land or to people and culture, were a direct result of settler colonialism and *not* of Indigenous agency (or a combination of the two and a variety of other factors). Therefore, my goal here is simply to centralize those of Indigenous heritage and to explore myself, other arrivants, and settlers in relationship to them and this place. When First Nations scholar Daniel Heath Justice was in my homeland, he said, "When I am a guest of the Kanaka Maoli in Hawai'i, that is the center of the world, for it is their world."[21] This type of shift in thinking to consider "host" and "guest" relationships is echoed in Jo Smith's work. In examining Pākehā, Māori, and migrant in Aotearoa/New Zealand (representing settler, Indigenous, and arrivant respectively), she argues that a "host-guest model" can help in challenging "the state's role as 'host' to immigrants" while also exposing it "as usurper of customary rights casting out *tangata whenua* [Māori] as originary host."[22] Thinking of this model and my current position as an arrivant in Aotearoa, and as a guest on land that is not my own, my scholarship here does (and must) recognize the originary host by centralizing Māori world(s).

This is my kuleana, or my responsibility, not only to other peoples who identify as Indigenous but also to Kahiki and the genealogical relationships we share across our ocean.

Settler Colonialism

When I attended NAISA 2019 and spoke about my positionality in Aotearoa and my responsibilities to this place, an older woman in the audience raised her hand and asked about my terminology. I quickly learned that she was from Hawai'i. After commenting on the fact that she doesn't hear people use terms like "settler colonialism" at home, she asked me to explain it and then asked whether or not she needs to use it. Her question was a lesson for me in how essential it is to provide our peoples with the language to articulate their experiences of oppression. This is why Tina and I spoke about the Doctrine of Discovery. It was to provide words and frameworks for talking about why we continue to suffer as Indigenous Pacific peoples. "Colonialism" is a common word in many conversations in Hawai'i. "Settler colonialism," however, is still new for some people, especially people like the woman in the audience, perhaps of my mother's generation, who felt like she had missed something. Therefore, unpacking "settler colonialism" and examining its ongoing impacts on us today is essential.[23]

In the 1990s, Patrick Wolfe made important distinctions between colonialism and settler colonialism, one of the most crucial being settler colonialism's continuity. In his often-quoted phrase, he asserted that it is "a structure not an event." Settler colonizers, he argues, "come to stay" with the goal of accessing and gaining territory, which comes with the inevitability of Indigenous displacement or disappearance.[24] The mission of territoriality is accomplished through what he terms the "logic of elimination" or the "settler-colonial tendency" to eliminate the Indigenous, sometimes through outright genocide, and at other times in the form of a more devious strategy that does not always lead to physical death.[25] While my work uses this logic to unravel and expose some of the ways events like Tuia 250 enable the continued disappearance of Indigenous peoples and histories, Wolfe's singular logic has been, and must be, critiqued. In their work "Writing Indigenous Histories" and "Indigenous Heterogeneity," Miranda Johnson and Tim Rowse call for reading settler colonialism, as Rowse describes, as being "less predictable, messier, more surprising and occasionally more hopeful."[26] Their work challenges the so-called inevitability or predictability of settler colonialism and Wolfe's singular logic. It argues that settler colonialism is not a single structure but several "contending structures," and that in our examinations of these structures, we must account for Indigenous agency and the many diverse ways it is exercised and expressed.[27] Therefore, while this chapter *will* examine different logics of elimination, it will also account for some of the "messier" and even "more hopeful" ways settler colonialism is encountered, reacted to, and resisted.

To examine settler colonialism, and to further challenge Wolfe's singular logic, we must also recognize the centrality of space, both physical and ideological. In his study of Antarctica, Adrian Howkins argues that space and an ongoing control of space—and *not* the elimination of people—is paramount to the settler colonial project: "The struggle against Indigenous peoples was not central to settler colonialism; rather it was an unwelcome distraction from the central goal of appropriating space."[28] In fact, he frames Antarctica as the "ideal settler colony" because there were no people for competing countries to deal with when trying to claim territory there. If the "ideal" is not what is encountered upon arrival, therefore, then people become casualties in the process of taking and controlling space. This is perhaps what is most disturbing about the centralization of space in the settler colonial project: it is the idea that people do not matter, and that "if people do not matter, then what happens to them does not matter either."[29] This racist assumption has roots in the Doctrine of Discovery and is the reason Tina and I talked about it at Ihumātao. Thus, in the case of Tuia 250, I will argue that people *do* matter and that they have to matter, especially in the ways that they are being positioned in relation to history. The positioning of Indigenous peoples, settlers, and arrivants matters in the way it solidifies the settler state's control of physical space, while simultaneously allowing for its continued manipulation and dominance of ideological spaces as well.

Tuia—Encounters 250

Tuia 250 was (and though the events have finished, continues to be) a contentious, heated, and antagonizing space. Its name, however, seems to suggest otherwise. As explained on the official website, "Tuia means 'to weave or bind together' and is drawn from a whakataukī (proverb) and karakia (ritual chant) that refers to the intangible bonds established between people when they work together."[30] While "tuia" seems to imply that there can be a neat weaving together of ideas, histories, and values, what resulted in the commemorative events was far messier, pricklier, and painful. In fact, in the months before its launch in October 2019, Tuia 250 stabbed at old, unhealed wounds, inciting reaction and staunch resistance. Through strategic word choice, organizers used its full name, Tuia—Encounters 250, to try and bring a Māori word and a European concept together, seeking both to Indigenize the settler and to promote a kind of historical amnesia, while also promoting the idea that healing old wounds would be possible if everyone worked together.

The naming of Tuia 250 was therefore anything but innocent; it was, and is, political. Naming, as Amanda Murphyao and Kelly Black explain, "is not static . . . it is part of an ongoing process of legitimizing access to land and resources."[31] While they were speaking about place names specifically, their argument can be extended to the naming of other things as well. Tuia—Encounters 250, for example, sought to legitimize settler colonial access and control of physical and ideological spaces in this country. By employing the use of a Māori word, the event could pass itself off as being sympathetic to Māori culture—or perhaps even appearing to honor it—while also seeking to promote Aotearoa New Zealand as a "bicultural" society. In the process of combining "tuia" with "encounters," the name normalized settler presence, putting the Māori and the European together on equal grounding, assuming that their histories began at the same time, strands apparently being woven together since first contact. The name worked to secure for the settler a physical and ideological space. In doing so, the settler state could further entrench itself into the landscape of Aotearoa, while simultaneously reimagining and rewriting history, both by leaving key facts out and by appropriating Indigenous language to "create a distinctive 'New Zealand' culture."[32] All of this was done with the goal of legitimizing the role of the settler state and its control of not only *what* and *who* gets remembered (or not), but *how* and *why* as well.

The naming of Tuia 250 also implied that there was opportunity for reconciliation and understanding. This was, in fact, one of the goals of the event. According to the Tuia 250 website, "This is a time to share, debate and reflect—to enable a more balanced telling of our stories, so that we speak openly and respectfully about our history. *Tuia 250* is an opportunity to hold some honest conversations about Māori and European settlement of New Zealand to guide us as we go forward together."[33] The mere proposal that there could be peaceful, mutually beneficial conversations about history denies the fact that, as Wolfe articulated years ago, settler colonialism is not an event; it is an ongoing structure. Cook's landing and subsequent murders at Tūranganui-a-Kiwa, and later elsewhere, are not something that can be simply forgiven at a commemorative event. In fact, as Cavanagh explains, we cannot talk about the devastating impacts of settler colonialism, and the harm suffered at first "encounter," in the past tense.[34] They are not finished. There can be no reconciliation, in other words, until we recognize how the "encounter" celebrated did not lead to equal benefits for all involved. The "encounter," in fact, is ongoing and has had, and continues to have, destructive impacts that must be reckoned with. Any assumption that Tuia 250 could be an opportunity to talk about "settlement" in the past tense suggests that the settler colonial state has finished settling, which would signal its ultimate success. If people believe this and accept the false idea that colonial injustices reside only in the past, we will have no real chance at addressing settler colonial injustices as they continue to unfold in the present.

Unsettling the Settler

Fortunately, the settler colonial state cannot completely "settle" or solidify its place while it is being resisted and while its logics of deception and elimination are being made visible. In addition to speaking publically in resistance to Tuia 250, opponents published critiques, provided statements to news outlets, created and displayed art, did extensive research, boycotted the event, and engaged in dialogue about the hurt invoked by it. Tina also took concerns to the United Nations, lodging a complaint, as the New Zealand government planned to launch a "First Encounters" program in schools.[35] Actively opposing Tuia 250 since she first learned about it in 2014, Tina was (and continues to be) firm in her commitment to educating others about the histories that were being, and are still, ignored. Additionally, while not speaking directly to the motives driving those Māori who *were* choosing to participate in the commemorations, she unpacked what their participation meant.[36] In a blog post titled "Why I Won't Give the Cook Celebrations My Brown-ness," she unraveled the complexities of complicity, or of what participating in the celebrations as Māori could contribute to the further settling of colonialism. Among her reasons for boycotting and resisting Tuia 250, she states, "I will not be a tool of defence for our colonial government."[37] In other words, she understood that her attendance at the events, or the attendance of any "brown" person, could be used to "signal to ourselves, and the world, that our interests are being represented and supported. In this sense—it doesn't really matter *what* is said in our participation—what counts is that we participated."[38] That participation, she argued, is precisely what could be twisted and reframed as Indigenous acceptance and be used to defend the commemorations if and when they were critiqued.

Vocal opponents of Tuia 250 such as Tina, Moana Jackson, and Robyn Kahukiwa continually disturbed the settler, shaking the colonial structure, through their resistance.[39] Essentially, every question they posed and every challenge they generated in opposition to what attempted to be normalized was part of a necessary process of unsettling settler colonialism. Jackson, for instance, wrote about the danger of monuments for what they "reveal and conceal," arguing that they signal what and who is worth knowing and remembering. The commemorative events for Cook functioned as a sort of monument, perhaps not in the physical sense, but in the way they erected a moment and carved a space in history for remembering while also, as Jackson explains, promoting a "seemingly unchangeable reality that needs neither justification nor explanation."[40] Through Tuia 250, Cook's "presence" in history as the first to encounter tangata whenua—and serve as a gateway to a bicultural New Zealand—was solidified and given a sort of permanence as a "milestone" to be celebrated. While Tuia 250 purported to provide space for critical engagement with Cook's coming to Aotearoa, it actually accomplished the opposite, centralizing him and assuming that his landing here was something worth commemorating in the first place. Cook's presence, therefore, must be continually challenged, interpreted, and reinterpreted. Rather than celebrating his arrival as a landmark in history, in other words, and positioning him like a statue in time, stuck, permanent, or unmovable, he must be engaged with as a marker of settler colonialism and subsequently disassembled.

Cook

Amid all of the controversy and debate, I had to consider my positionality. If something like Tuia 250 happened in Hawai'i, I would be wholly opposed to it as a Kanaka Maoli. Since I was in Aotearoa when the events occurred, however, I had to think about what my opposition meant as an arrivant. This kind of reflection is essential if we as Hawaiians are going to act upon our Kahiki connections, especially when we are in "Kahiki." As someone who is not tangata whenua, I therefore thought it imperative that I also resist lending my brownness to Tuia 250. Though I am not from this land, and while my ancestors were not among those killed at Tūranganui-a-Kiwa, I believe I have a responsibility to "center Māori worlds," and to decentralize colonial narratives in the process. Quite simply, if I am not standing against settler colonialism and its tactics to distort history, or to try to reconcile what cannot be reconciled without drastic change, and if I am not prioritizing and privileging the stories of those who were already here over those who came later, then I am part of the problem. This knowing meant that I had to help shoulder the burden of the commemorative event by making its underlying, colonial motives visible and making its problems known. Further, this knowing also meant that I must continue to dismantle settler colonial structures every day.

To do so, I have chosen to draw on Cook himself, the captain whose life ended thousands of miles away in my homeland of Hawai'i in 1779, ten years after his landing in Aotearoa. In choosing to look at his death, however, it is not the goal of this chapter to examine what led to his demise, especially since there has long been speculation about what actually happened on the beach in Kealakekua, Hawai'i, where he was killed. Further, as Kerry Howe explains, interpretations of the events leading to his death often reveal more about the interpreter than about what actually happened. Each interpretation, he argues, "ultimately derives from a 'political' positioning that depends on how Cook and the Hawaiians are regarded."[41] Thus, rather that engage with those political statements, my aim is to create my own, fully acknowledging the fact that I cannot, and do not intend to, ignore my own political positioning as a Hawaiian and as an Indigenous woman. I am aware of my bias, for example, as someone who wants to unravel the apparent "tuia," or weaving together of histories (not just in the actual Tuia 250 events but also in the ongoing attempts of settler governments to do so), to see what they can offer us as we move toward decolonization, not just in Aotearoa or Hawaiʻi but around the Pacific and the world as well.

Rather than focus on Cook's death, therefore, or on the many debates about whether or not he was considered to be a god by Hawaiians[42]—something that has been written about extensively by Marshall Sahlins and Gananath Obeyesekere and carefully reviewed by Howe[43]—I will focus on what happened afterward. In 1823, missionary William Ellis toured the island of Hawaiʻi. One of the places he visited on his journey was Kealakekua Bay. In his writing about the area, he reflects on what he learned during his visit to the "spot where the body of the unfortunate Captain Cook was cut to pieces, and the flesh, after being separated from the bones, was burnt."[44] In his biography of Captain Cook, John Cawte Beaglehole confirms the dismembering and burning of Cook's body. According to his research, a piece of flesh from the captain's thigh was returned to his ship the day after he was killed, the rest of the flesh having been burnt. At the time, captain Charles Clerke had taken command of the ship and demanded that they receive the rest of Cook's remains. According to Beaglehole, the next day a procession of Hawaiians brought a bundle to Clerke:

> It contained . . . the scalp, all the long bones, thighs, legs, arms, and the skull; the jawbone of the latter was missing, as were the feet, and the hands were separate. All had been scraped clean except the hands, which had been preserved with salt and stuffed into a number of gashes . . . . The backbone and ribs had been consumed with the flesh in the fire. The following morning the chief came again, brining the jawbone and the feet, together with Cook's shoes and the bent and battered barrels of his musket. The remains were put into a coffin, and late in the afternoon of this day, 21 February, amid all the marks of naval grief . . . they were sunk in the waters of the bay.[45]

According to reports, the remains of Cook's crew who were also killed that day were distributed among different chiefs and therefore could not be returned to the ship with some (but not all) of their captain.

I focus on the dismemberment and partial "return" of Cook's bones to his crew because I believe it serves as a suitable metaphor for what must be done in settler colonial contexts. In short, settler colonialism must be dismembered, taken apart, and revealed piece by piece. This is especially important when settler colonialism is mistaken as "internal colonialism," or inequality experienced by, and oppression enacted upon, minorities *within* a nation. In the United States, Byrd explains, "the idea of 'internal colonialism' services the construction of the United States as a multicultural nation that is struggling with the legacies of racism rather than as a colonialist power engaged in territorial expansion since its beginning."[46] In Aotearoa, internal colonialism positions Māori as another minority group, thereby threatening (and attempting to extinguish) their status as tangata whenua with prior claims to place.

In the case of Tuia 250, and exacerbating the issue, was the fact that it fed on the assumption that Māori are just another ethnic group in a multicultural society, meant to discuss and negotiate their right to space with settlers and arrivants (though it should be mentioned that the Tuia 250 website emphasized biculturalism, giving little to no space to arrivants, thus leaving us to question if we have a role here). The commemoration, therefore, essentially masqueraded as "internal," or as something to be shared by two entities that are both from *within* New Zealand. This made debates, boycotts, and protests appear to be an issue of a Māori minority seeking recognition of their historical and current grievances by a European majority, both equal and inherent parts of the New Zealand nation. Conflict surrounding Tuia 250 had to be framed this way so as not to call into question "settlers' attempts to assert their own cultural distinctiveness."[47] In other words, the commemoration could not reveal settlers as settlers because that would undermine its goal of normalizing them, giving the settler state space and distinction (via sprinklings of culture and small usages of the Indigenous language) to set themselves apart from other countries.

While discussing internal colonialism, Rohrer references a metaphor offered by Audra Simpson. In this metaphor, she explains that the "native people in North America have been 'ingested by Columbus'" to become "'the irritant that cannot be spoken of,' the 'unease in his entrails.'"[48] In the United States, the settler state, represented by Columbus, ingests the native—taking them in, making them another "other"—in order to deny their claims to place as first peoples. As the native continues to resist erasure and continues to call for sovereignty, however, they become the irritant, ensuring that "Columbus" (and all he represents) can never be fully comfortable or settled as he battles indigestion in the form of resistance.

In the context of Hawai'i, Rohrer makes clear that Cook cannot be used in the same way as Columbus, especially considering that he does not hold the same "national weight."[49] He can, however, still serve as a metaphor, not for the success of settler colonialism but rather the hopeful resistance to it. In Hawai'i, Cook did not "ingest" the natives. Instead, his body was taken apart, burnt, and stripped, and his bones were cleaned and dispersed. What was received by his crew was then sunk into the waters of Kealakekua. Therefore, unlike Columbus, he could not devour the native because he had no entrails to hold them. While the dismemberment of Cook's body can be seen as violent and perhaps read as cruel or "savage" (as it has been described), it is important to think about the process and not the single event. The process of stripping flesh and cleaning bones was a ceremonial one, one done with ritual and prayer. It was not careless. It was not thoughtless. It had intention. This process, I argue, represents precisely what is needed to continually unsettle settler colonialism. Whether we are Indigenous, arrivants, or settlers, I believe that we have the responsibility to dismember that which seeks to normalize itself. We have a duty to peel back the layers of possession, territoriality, and control, to expose it for what it is and to strip away whatever gets in the way of us seeing the bones, or the true intent and goals, of settler colonialism itself.

Kahiki as Sanctuary

When I presented my ideas at NAISA 2019, and talked about my positionality as an arrivant in Aotearoa, a fellow scholar in the audience asked why I did not draw on genealogies in my talk. What he asked, essentially, was why I did not use my Kahiki connections, or the fact that we are genealogically connected as Pacific peoples, to position myself in Aotearoa. My response was that I could not allow myself to be too comfortable here. I did not want to use Kahiki to justify my presence. Rather, I wanted to use Kahiki to inform my critical reflection of myself in this place. Thus, although in the background, Kahiki is what encouraged me to consider what it means to be in another place in the Pacific *now*. It forced me to pay attention to the particularities of this place, knowing that if I were in another part of the Pacific, I would have to orient myself again, knowing the concerns of those people, centering their worlds. This, to me, is what it means to be in Kahiki, not just in name, not just in genealogy, but in everyday practice.

Coming here to Aotearoa, I have reflected on Simpson's Columbus metaphor to see what I, as a Kanaka Maoli, can bring to this country. My people in Hawai'i are not the irritant *in* Cook because we were not ingested by him. Instead, we dismembered him, took him apart, separating his bones, so that he could not exist whole. Thus, in Hawai'i, we can control where, when, and why he appears or doesn't, bringing him out in bundles when necessary. It is this practice of selection that I believe I can bring to Aotearoa, and is what I feel I can offer as an arrivant. Living here as a Hawaiian, as someone who is not tangata whenua but who often occupies liminal spaces, I can lend my voice, my actions, and my protest in support of Māori to continue what my people did: taking him apart with intention, digging into the skin of settler colonialism and revealing it for what it is and for what it does. I don't claim to have any right to space here in Aotearoa. What I do know, however, is that *if* I am going to be in this space I have to be mindful of how I position myself and of what that positionality means. This is part of what it means to be an Indigenous ally, or someone who centers the worlds of the people whose lands they are on and fights for their sovereignty, at their side. Tuia 250 was, and still is, an insult to tangata whenua and to all other Pacific peoples who have been affected by, and who continue to feel the impacts of, settler colonialism, of which Cook is a primary symbol. Therefore, my hope is that settlers and arrivants alike recognize this and choose to disassemble that which seeks to exist whole and normal, stripping it to its bones. As long as I act upon my Kahiki connections to this land, I know that I will continue to hold myself accountable to the place in which I now reside, implicating myself in the settler colonial project, admitting how I've benefitted from it, and never allowing myself, my presence, or my genealogical comfort to be part of the problem.

6

IN KAHIKI THERE IS LIFE

Kahiki and Dreaming

I like to think of myself as a dreamer, as someone who has visions in mind of what I'd like the future to look like. I don't see "dreaming" as fantasy building or escaping reality. Rather, I see it as necessary to fuel our movements in the *now*. In various conversations had during 2019, I noticed a recurring query about the post-, the afterward: a journal editor asked me to envision a postplastic future; a friend prompted me to think about a post–Doctrine of Discovery future; and as our stand to protect Mauna Kea continues, I still find myself in discussions about a post–Thirty Meter Telescope (TMT) future. What I noticed in these conversations is that it's sometimes a struggle to imagine, to dream, down to the tiniest details, what our worlds will look like, sound like, taste like, or feel like in the "after." My friend who asked about the Doctrine of Discovery (explored in the previous chapter) wanted to know what I saw myself waking up to in the morning, where I'd spend my days, what I'd spend my time doing. She wanted me to picture a world where we did not have to fight against the enduring assumptions promoted by the doctrine: white supremacy, the inferiority of Indigenous peoples, and the so-called right of conquest. To be honest, when she asked, I struggled to respond. I had to think hard, and I still wonder if what I said then was a true visioning of the future. What would our world be like without that layer of hate and prejudice that has plagued so many of our lives for so long? At the time, I didn't really know what would wake me up in the morning; I only knew what I didn't want to wake up to: more hate, more pain, more destruction, more injustice.

As a teacher, I try to encourage my students to know not only what they are fighting against but also what they are fighting for. I want them to be like the great leaders of our pasts who "dared to talk openly of revolution and dream of a new society . . . to envision what's possible with collective action, personal self-transformation, and will."[1] Even in doing so, however, I've realized that I sometimes limit my own dreaming to the now, not truly allowing it to move into the after. My envisionings of a Pacific futurity in chapter 3 are an example of this; they focus more on what I'm fighting against, or dreaming against, than on what I'm fighting or dreaming for. I dream of the TMT not being built. I dream of sacred lands being saved. I dream of waterways being restored. I dream of the end of racism. But then what? What happens after that, long after that, in a time when the mere idea of a telescope on a sacred mountain is ridiculous, when the mere suggestion of taking Indigenous land from Indigenous people is immediately thrown out, and when anyone proposing to revive something as destructive as the long-abandoned plastic industry is quickly turned down? To dream, I learned in my conversations in 2019, is to go there, far beyond what is now, so that we can engage in the work of creating those futures in the present.

Even in the beauty of dreaming, however, and the consolation it brings to my heart in a world full of so much devastation (environmental and otherwise), I've also learned that our dreams of the future will be shaped by how we experience the present (or how our orientations in the world shape the way we experience it). Though this seems obvious, what perhaps isn't always considered is the fact that there are multiple presents existing simultaneously. That's where dreaming gets complicated and where dreaming can be dangerous. The mayor of the Big Island of Hawai'i, Harry Kim, for example, has been called a "dreamer." He's been known to talk about feelings and about hearts and souls. He's been known to have vision, to look to the future. However, his dreams come from *his* present, which is not the one I experience every day, and not the one many of our kia'i experience every day either. As the common phrase goes, and as I've heard people say in reference to him, "He's in another world." While this could imply that he's off somewhere, lost in daydreams, here it means, quite literally, that he experiences the world in very different ways. This is not to say, of course, that temporalities cannot and do not overlap, or that there is one distinct Indigenous existence in time and one distinct non-Indigenous existence in time that never interact. Instead, as Mark Rifkin explains, our worlds are full of "discrepant temporalities that can be understood as affecting each other, as all open to change, and yet as not equivalent or mergeable into a neutral, common frame."[2] Mayor Kim's experience of the *now* and his subsequent dreams for the future are not only unmergeable with my own but, if fulfilled, will render my dreams impossible. This is the predicament of dreaming: we all have dreams, but the opportunity for those dreams to come true is often dependent on dominant colonial temporalities that always exist on uneven ground with others.

In February 2018, Mayor Kim shared his dreams for Mauna Kea. An article printed in the *Hawaiʻi Tribune-Herald* opens by saying, "When it comes to Maunakea, Mayor Harry Kim might seem like a dreamer. But he's counting on not being the only one."[3] This was in response to Kim's plan to organize a Mauna Kea committee to "pursue *his* [emphasis added] vision of the mountain as a symbol of international cooperation, the pursuit of knowledge and the Hawaiian people," a dream he still maintains.[4] Kim has been a decided supporter of the TMT, and is quoted in the article as saying that he will be sad (for both Hawaiʻi and the world) if it is not built on our mauna. While calling for people to be sensitive and to have compassion for Kānaka Maoli, Kim both advocates for the construction of the TMT—seeing it as a critical component of his vision—while also talking about creating both a "major cultural center and gathering place" and opportunities to "participate in efforts to integrate culture and nature in heritage protection."[5] Recognizing the significance of Mauna Kea and acknowledging the connection many Kānaka have to the mountain, he then attempts to show care and concern while simultaneously stomping on our dreams: "'If you're going to develop this place for science,' Kim said he told UH [University of Hawaiʻi] officials, 'please remember that to a lot people, this is not a place for science, that this is a part of their soul. And if you're going to trample on their soul, please do it with care[,] with caution and compassion.'"[6] In Kim's world, it is okay to destroy someone's soul as long as you do it nicely. In Kim's world, you can construct an eighteen-story telescope in one of the most pristine and fragile environments while also talking about nature and heritage protection, perhaps not seeing that ʻāina, that place, is integral to heritage. In Kim's world, our dreams cannot exist because they run counter to his own. Therefore, he attempts to dream for us: to propose a cultural center to appease us, to acknowledge the intelligence of our kūpuna to honor us, and to say that his vision will "bring world recognition of the Hawaiians, their achievement as well as the wrongs (done to them)," as if recognition and true reconciliation are the same thing.[7]

What Kim's statements show us, therefore, is that while we all have the capacity to dream, some of us have to work so much harder to see our dreams come true. In this chapter, the final chapter of this book, I will examine settler colonial articulations of time and space in order to present Indigenous counterparts that may be better suited for planting and nurturing our dreams. To do so, this chapter will look at the colonial domestication of Indigenous spatialities and temporalities as attempts to restrict the building of futures by confining people either to the past or to a singular present that does not accommodate our experiences of the world. To work through this, I will propose that Kahiki, as a sanctuary and as the nonphysical space from which life comes, is the ultimate expression of Indigenous space and time, one that cannot be colonized, one that cannot be coopted, and even one that cannot be trampled on, no matter the amount of compassion shown in the process. It is my hope here to renew and reinvigorate Kahiki as a space where we can always dream good dreams, a space where there are no limits on our imaginings of the future, and a space where any and all visions of a multitude of afterwards can exist.

Kahiki Orientations

In settler colonial time, the settler state is taken as a "given" in which the present unfolds. It therefore "functions as something of an atemporal container for the occurrences, movements, conjunctures, periodicities, and pulsations of history."[8] The assumption, then, is that whatever we do as Indigenous peoples within a state's territory also occurs within a present in which the settler state is the legitimate power, the Indigenous peoples are placed in relation to that power (usually marginalized and oppressed), and our movements together exist in a singular now. As Kānaka Maoli, many of us resist the idea that our incorporation into the United States was a "given," that our takeover was inevitable, and that our futures can exist only within state-sanctioned limits. Thus, as I've learned, if we truly want to dream, we have to also resist the domestication and colonization of our time. In other words, because a primary justification for colonization around the world relied upon the argument that peoples and places needed to be tamed and civilized, we cannot allow that same mentality to continue to infiltrate our spaces of dreaming in which we envision a future that is not only beyond colonial boundaries but also imagines what it may be like when those boundaries do not even exist.

The work of reorienting ourselves in space and time, however, is not easy when we know only of an existence that is tied to colonial powers. In Hawai'i, for instance, what does the world look like post-US occupation? What does the world look like postmilitarism? Can we even imagine such a world? I personally know that I want a future that is free of both. However, what exactly it will look, feel, taste, and sound like is something I still have to give myself permission to imagine. In order to do so, I believe it is essential to consider Kanaka Maoli orientations, or ways of positioning ourselves in space and time so that we can view our worlds (and hopefully, our futures) differently. Kahiki, as the ever-evolving and generative concept at the center of this book, provides opportunity for us to do this work. Therefore, once again stretching back to knowledge recorded by kūpuna, I will attempt to reflect on some of our Indigenous orientations.

In "Mele a Pākuʻi," a genealogical chant telling of the creation of the universe and our islands, Kahiki appears in various forms, not as faraway lands but as parts of the atmosphere within a Kanaka world:

A [o] Wakea o Kahikoluamea—a—e
O Papa, o Papa-hanau-moku ka wahine
Hanau Kahiki-ku, Kahiki-moe
Hanau Keapapanuu
Hanau Hawaiʻi, he moku makahiapo
He keiki maka-hiapo a laua[9]
[And it was Wākea of Kahikoluamea
Papa, Papahānaumoku was the woman
Born was Kahikikū, Kahikimoe
Born was Keʻāpapanuʻu[10]
Born was Hawaiʻi, a first-born child
It was their eldest child].

The line "Hanau Kahiki-kū, Kahiki-moe," or "Born was Kahikikū, Kahikimoe," according to noted nineteenth-century historian David Malo, tells of the emergence of two layers of the atmosphere above earth: "'O kahi mai ka honua aku, a mai ka moana aku, e moe aku ana ma ka nānā ʻana aku a ka maka, a pili aku i ka ʻalihi aouli, ua kapa ʻia ʻo Kahiki-moe ia pōʻai [As for the area extending outward from the land and outward from the sea, laying where the eye traces the edge of the sky, this circle is called Kahiki-moe]."[11] And further, "'O ka ʻalihi aouli e hui ana me ka ʻalihi moana e piʻi aʻe ana i luna, ua kapa ʻia aku o Kahiki-kū ia pōʻai [As for where the edge of the sky meets with the edge of the sea, the portion just above this is called Kahiki-kū]."[12] "Kahikimoe" can therefore can be interpreted as "the horizon," and Kahikikū, as "the space of sky just above it."[13] Although interpretations of these zones sometimes disagree—in fact, another Kanaka historian, Joseph Poepoe, believed that Kahikikū and Kahikimoe were the names for two cardinal points,[14] Kahikikū being where the sun rises, or stands, in the east, and Kahikimoe where the sun sets, or lies down, in the west[15]—there seems to be some level of agreement that they refer to spaces that, although not tangible, seem to define "the limits of the visible from the Hawaiian archipelago."[16]

The root word in these two layers of the atmosphere—or as Kekuewa Kikiloi interprets them, these two points that "highlight boundaries that stretch to both east and west horizons"—is "Kahiki."[17] As explored in previous chapters, "Kahiki" is a complex term that was used in past generations to explain everything from ancestral origins in the Pacific to the existence of people and places beyond our sea of islands. Furthermore, according to Valerio Valeri, "Kahiki" refers to "all that is distant in time and space."[18] Thus, the names Kahikikū and Kahikimoe contain that same idea of "distance," or of being "out there," and thus perhaps mark a boundary between what is visible from the Hawaiian Islands—all the way to the horizon and the levels of the sky above it—and all that is not visible beyond those boundaries, located somewhere in Kahiki. Not being visible, however, does not imply a lack of knowledge or understanding, and it does not imply detachment. Kānaka Maoli, for instance, maintained memories of Kahiki long after they left it. After interarchipelago travel ceased, Kahiki continued to be an integral part of Kanaka genealogies. It was also seen as a life-giving place/space, one that gods and ancestors came from, and one that could continue to inspire and influence.[19] Therefore, although it may not have been seen, it was *known* as a sacred space residing beyond the edge of the sea and sky, beyond Kahikimoe, lying flat on the horizon, and Kahikikū curving into the dome of atmosphere just above it.

Important in the line of chant cited above is the fact that these two layers of the atmosphere are birthed; they are created. According to the mele (chant), it is Papa herself, the same woman credited with giving birth to the Hawaiian Islands and later to the first Kanaka (as discussed in chapter 1), who creates these regions. In terms of birth order, Kahikikū and Kahikimoe are older than the islands themselves, thus establishing the idea that their creation marked the limits of the visible world, forming the space within which Hawai'i itself could exist, and later, where Kānaka could be positioned at the center of that world. Thus, Kahiki, in its atmospheric forms, creates opportunities for "temporal orientation." In his book *Beyond Settler Time*, Rifkin explains, "Being temporally oriented suggests that one's experiences, sensations, and possibilities for action are shaped by the existing inclinations, itineraries, and networks in which one is immersed."[20] In a settler state such as Hawai'i, the danger is that if we are immersed in a system of hegemony and ongoing imperialism, our movements and actions within settler time and space may habitually and unconsciously reinforce settler colonial power. Thus, it is essential that we continue to orient ourselves in ways that do not rely on "dominant settler orderings, articulations, and reckonings of time," particularly those that seek to plot all of our movements and experiences in relation to "national" stories of progress.[21] Kahiki, both as a distant place and as the layers of the atmosphere, defies colonial time, thereby opening opportunities for understanding ourselves, and feeling ourselves, in space and time in more liberating ways.

Creating pō'ai, or circles at the edge of what is visible, Kahikikū and Kahikimoe ensure that no matter where we are, or where we go, we will always be able to understand ourselves in relation to them. The naming of places beyond land, as Katrina-Ann R. Kapā Oliveira explores in her book on

Hawaiian geographies, demonstrates that a Kanaka understanding of space encompassed "heavenscapes, landscapes, and oceanscapes" that were made into "personalized places."[22] Thus, Kahikikū and Kahikimoe were not just descriptors for distant entities but were also entities that Kānaka could engage with, even at a distance. Although appearing to be fixed in space, these layers of the sky were, and are, fluid and flexible. After all, their position depends on where we are at any given moment. The zone of Kahikimoe, positioned at the horizon, for example, moves as we move. With each step forward, it moves further away, shifting spaces and perspectives. With each step toward something or someone, we simultaneously leave things and peoples behind, changing our views and changing the possibilities of our interactions. As Kahikimoe moves with us, it ensures that we will never reach it. This, for me, means that we will never reach the limits of our own potential.

Drawing on Kahikikū and Kahikimoe, I believe they enable us to escape the confines of colonial spatialities and temporalities. These regions, for example, do not exist in linear time, moving in one direction. They are at once as ancient as time itself and also constantly being made new with every step we take toward or away from them. They change constantly. Therefore, as long as we know ourselves as existing within the pōʻai they create, we will never be locked into a time that is limited, controlled, or domesticated by the colonial state. This also means that experiences in space and time are individualized, depending on my own personal interactions with the pōʻai around me, thus resisting any attempt to frame time as being singular, unified, or dependent on the so-called inevitability of colonial dominance. Like the stories and genealogies they come from, Kahikikū and Kahikimoe move and change. They grow and expand as much as they constantly bend back and into themselves. It is within this space, a space of circular time, that I want to dream, because it is where the past, present, and future interact, and where Kānaka Maoli will always be able to orient themselves/ourselves to the standing and resting Kahiki at the edge of all that is visible.

A Peace Park

While Kahikikū and Kahikimoe present opportunities for me to dream of a future beyond colonial limits, I know I must still contend with those "dreams" that are born *in* colonial time and that take colonial space as a given. Mayor Kim's dreams cited earlier, for example, are those that are given more settler-sanctioned time, as in media coverage, than those dreamt by kiaʻi.[23] Back in July 2017, Kim introduced the idea of a "peace park" "to celebrate the pursuit of knowledge, Hawaiian culture and the cosmopolitan makeup of Hawaiʻi's people."[24] He also added that he felt that Mauna Kea "could be an international monument for the aboriginal people of Australia, for the indigenous people all over the world."[25] What is not only problematic but also completely absurd about this latter statement is that Kim once again attempts to dream for us, for Kānaka *and* for Aboriginal Australians and other Indigenous peoples as well. What this implies is that we need him to create visions for us because we cannot do it for ourselves. This assumption locks us into a past in which Indigenous peoples are always seen as backward, antiprogressive, and therefore dependent upon the forward-thinking and forward-moving settler to go anywhere. What this also implies is that Hawaiian culture (most often seen and used by the state as a static, unchanging bundle of traits and customs) can be celebrated only so long as it does not interfere with the scientific pursuit of knowledge through telescopes and what he believes to be a "multicultural" Hawai'i in which Kānaka Maoli are just another ethnic minority (the problems of which have been discussed in the previous chapter). This is not the dream I have for our mauna, and while I will not pretend that the dreams of kia'i are at all homogenous, I can say with certainty that any vision that still allows for the construction of the TMT and the protection of state efforts to colonize and control our sacred spaces is not only unacceptable but will be resisted with everything we have.

Though the strategic use of the word "peace" may suggest otherwise, Kim's visions are violent; they are emblematic of settler colonial conceptualizations of Indigenous space as places to be taken, tamed, controlled, and exploited. In her study of the appropriation of Indigenous lands, Tracey Banivanua-Mar examines national parks as being instrumental in the colonial project to develop spaces that can be deemed as examples of "progress" in order to simultaneously empty them of Indigenous presence.[26] National parks and wildlife refuges, after all, can be see as progressive in that they claim to protect nature. However, as Banivanua-Mar explains, "The creation of national parks as bordered wilderness and nature reserves represents the pinnacle of settler colonialism's rush for land . . . [or] the imagined completion of settler colonial land projects" because it suggests that the state has all the land it needs and can therefore mark its excess in the form of parks while also simultaneously setting up borders that Indigenous peoples cannot cross into for dwelling.[27]

In the case of Mauna Kea, Kānaka Maoli never did (and still do not) live on the uppermost levels of the mountain. Those spaces are considered wao akua, or the realm of gods, and are therefore far too sacred for human dwelling. What Kim's peace park proposes, then, is not necessarily to empty the mountain of Kanaka inhabitants but to mark the space as a colonial possession by attempting to empty it of spiritual value—as a place Hawaiians connect to genealogically and visit to hold ceremonies honoring gods and goddesses, praying for water and life—and by ascribing it with new state-imposed significance as a scientific hub for exploration. Important to note is that kia'i are against *all* construction on the summit, whether that of a thirty-meter telescope or a cultural center. Anything that disrupts the sanctity of the mountain and that must dig into the soil or dig into hillsides and destroy fragile environments is intolerable. Kim's peace park, then, is nothing but a poor attempt to mask the violence and destruction of the TMT with talks of peace, as if they could appease kiaʻi. What Kim fails to realize is that peace, true peace, does not need a physical space within which to be cultivated. It does not need a park, in other words, on the summit of a sacred mountain.

Another highly troublesome aspect of Kim's proposal is that it still places power in the hands of the colonial state, meaning that the government can do what it wants with the space once it establishes it as a state park. Parks, and in particular those that have been registered as historic places or nature reserves, can be manipulated to serve state agendas. Therefore, in some instances, what are established as spaces dedicated to the protection of historical or natural treasures are in fact settler-colonial reserves (or spaces of excess) to be used/abused when needed. In Guåhan (Guam), for example, Tiara Naʻputi and Michael Lujan Bevacqua discuss the ancient village of Pågat, which has been registered as a place of archaeological and historical significance in the Guam National Register of Historic Places. As they explain, Pågat is "one of the eleven most endangered historic places [and] . . . one of the 'last remaining and best preserved pre-colonial site[s] owned by the Government of Guam,' offering one of the most tangible connections to the island's ancient past."[28] Despite its deep cultural, historical, and spiritual significance, however, the US Department of Defense (DOD) still identified the area as a proposed location for a new live firing training complex in 2010. Importantly, despite being recognized and registered as a significant site, the DOD claimed that it chose Pågat because "it met all of the requirements for Marine training."[29] In other words, military training for the benefit of the colonial power takes priority over environmental protection, cultural significance, and even Indigenous well-being. This is an example of what Craig Santos Perez calls "the logic of military conservation." "You see," he explains, "designating land and water as a monument, refuge, reserve, or even sanctuary keeps the land under federal control as opposed to public (and indigenous) trust. So if the military wants to use the land in the future, it can simply be converted."[30] After a lawsuit was filed by We Are Guåhan, an organization dedicated to fighting the proposed US military buildup on the island, in partnership with the National Trust for Historic Preservation and the Guam Preservation Trust, the DOD started considering alternative locations.[31] This, however, has caused other problems in other places and continues to speak to the incredibly damaging militarization and occupation of Indigenous lands by the US military.

Though Kim's peace park is not being proposed as a site for military training, we cannot use the idea of "peace" as confirmation that what he envisions for the mauna will not be damaging and incredibly violent. As proven in statements with the press, and as cited earlier, Kim acknowledges that to build on the mountain, whether a TMT or a cultural park, is to "trample a people's soul." He's already established that trampling is fine as long as it is done nicely (as if that's a possibility). Therefore, his dream that the mauna be "a beacon of hope for the world" is really just *his* hope for *his* world, one in which we cannot exist as long as we are resistant to the settler colonial vision that relies upon our erasure.[32] Kim and David Ige, Hawai'i's governor, repeatedly speak about compromise, about coming to an agreement with which everyone can be happy. They talk about working together. However, as long as they insist on existing in colonial times and spaces that continue to subjugate Indigenous peoples and desecrate sacred places, there can be no compromise. Even a proposed peace park can be seen as an act of violence if it supports and allows for the desecration of our mountain, the continued disrespect of Kānaka Maoli, the denial of our beliefs and practices, and the shattering of our "souls."

A Puʻuhonua

Implicit in Kim's proposed park is the colonial need to mark possessions. Aileen Moreton-Robinson has written extensively on "white possession," arguing that it actually takes a lot of work to maintain possessions through "a process of perpetual Indigenous dispossession."[33] In her work, she therefore explains that colonial dominance must be marked, must be visible, and must be ubiquitous.[34] Interestingly, as it becomes more and more visible—in every street sign with a colonial name, in every colonial flag, in every government building, and in every structure that displaces another Indigenous person—that possession becomes more and more invisible, thus enabling the hegemonic endurance of the state. The peace park is yet another attempt to "mark" the mountain as a colonial space in the ongoing mission of the settler state to "settle," or to entrench itself into the landscape, into the history, and into the future of Hawai'i. As the primary goal of settler colonialism is the acquisition and maintenance of territory, marking it is essential in this process. What disrupts it, then, is when Indigenous peoples assert their sovereignty and act outside of spaces that have been demarcated for them/us.

A perfect example of radical sovereignty (a concept explored in chapter 3) is Puʻuhonua o Puʻuhuluhulu. As discussed in the introduction to this book, on July 13, 2019 (ahead of Governor Ige's designation of July 15 as the start date for TMT construction), the area of Puʻuhuluhulu, located at the base of Mauna Kea, was designated a puʻuhonua, or a sanctuary for all kiaʻi. This was not the first or only time a modern puʻuhonua had been established. After the seizure of Mākua Valley on the island of Oʻahu by the US military in 1941, a series of sweeps were conducted to remove people (mostly Kānaka) from the ʻāina. Kalamaokaʻāina Niheu explains that four separate "clearances" took places in 1964, 1977, 1983, and 1996, with the state declaring (in most cases) that their intention was to improve access to the area, to establish a state park, and to remove squatters. "The issue of public access," she clarifies, "has been repeatedly used as a wedge to isolate and vilify the peoples of Mākua, limit support by the general public, delegitimize any claim to the land by the residents, and obscure the primary motivation of keeping the land clear for military exercises."[35] In response to their being cleared from the land in the 1983 sweep, some of the residents who returned to Mākua declared it a "modern puʻuhonua" that was "open to anyone who needed sanctuary."[36]

Similar to what is unfolding on Mauna Kea, especially considering Kim's dreams for the mountain, the state pushed for the creation of a park at Mākua. Attempting to mask its true motives by proposing something of supposed benefit to the wider public of Hawaiʻi, the state used the park as further justification for the alienation of people from their lands. Thus, what Kim proposed in 2017, and what he continues to envision today, even as I write this, has a precedent in Mākua. His colonial tactics are nothing new. Fortunately, as Kānaka Maoli, we also have precedents. Ours, however, like Mākua, are those of strength, resistance, resilience, and sanctuary. Unlike the sanctuaries the state creates, such as natural reserves and wildlife parks that still serve and maintain settler colonial power, however, our puʻuhonua are about providing time and space for regeneration. Rather than being founded on settler logics of elimination that must displace the Indigenous, our sanctuaries are based on emplacement, or on reorienting people to place, to their rights *in* place, and, perhaps most importantly, to their ability to act, hope, and dream outside of state-sanctioned spatialities and singular temporalities.

What is perhaps the most powerful and telling difference between state-created parks and puʻuhonua, however, is that one is predicated on violence while the other is centered in love. Puʻuhonua o Puʻuhuluhulu, for example, has as its first and most important expectation the upholding of kapu aloha. As cited by Manulani Meyer, kapu aloha is "the reverence and practice of compassion."[37] It is a commitment to nonviolent action. It is a dedication to behaving in only the most respectful of ways. It is, as my cousin Pua Case often says, the recognition that a sacred place like Mauna Kea deserves and requires "sacred conduct." As such, the puʻuhonua has never been closed off or exclusionary. In fact, Governor Ige, Mayor Kim, and David Lassner, the president of the University of Hawaiʻi system (the current lease holder for the mountain), have all visited the puʻuhonua. Upon arrival, they have all been greeted, welcomed, and invited to listen, to share, and to learn. Our sanctuary at Puʻu Huluhulu therefore reinforces the fact that our Indigenous futurities do not depend upon the exclusion of settlers. If those state leaders were willing to truly immerse themselves in the sanctuary and learn from the kūpuna there about the need to protect our ʻāina—and that such protection can come from reorienting oneself, humbling oneself, and loving the natural world like an ancestor—then they could find a place next to us, dreaming of a future that is healthy, that is fair, and that is based on love and not violence.

However, if the settler state is to survive, then its leaders cannot dream *with* us. They must dream *for* us because the Indigenous cannot continue to exist in a settler futurity, one premised on the "expansive dispossession" of the Indigenous peoples that "dispossess[es] Indigenous communities of their futures—futures imagined on their terms within their ways of knowing."[38] This is why Puʻuhonua o Puʻuhuluhulu is so revolutionary. Not only is it a space that was created by Kānaka and unsanctioned by the state, but every day it is there, and every day it grows, it becomes a bigger threat to colonial powers. When police forces stood on the mauna in full riot gear on July 17, 2019, they stood as symbols of violence, armed as if they would have to protect themselves from unruly and wild kiaʻi. As countless videos and photos from that day prove, however, they were greeted only with love. On that day, they arrested thirty-three kūpuna, some with canes and walkers, some in wheelchairs. They bound their hands in zip ties even while their only response was to cry, to chant, or to sing. On that day, the world therefore witnessed that colonial violence does not know what to do with Indigenous love. It doesn't know what to do when those opposing them do not respond in, or with, violence. Thus, on that day, we witnessed the profound power of kapu aloha, something that transcends every attempt by the state to lock us into the antiquated and racist role of peoples needing to be tamed or civilized. The fierce and unwavering aloha shown that day has only carried on and expanded, not just at the puʻuhonua but also throughout the pae ʻāina (archipelago), and to other parts of the world. It is powerful, it is beautiful, and it is a future being dreamed and created in the now.

Since being established, the puʻuhonua has been visited by thousands of people, many coming from the Hawaiian Islands, but many also coming from the United States and even further abroad. Visiting the sanctuary, one will see flags flying from countries around the world. Kahiki is therefore at the mauna. The reach and impact of the puʻuhonua has been so immense that it has called people to it. However, while the sanctuary will continue to exist indefinitely, the large human presence in that space is not meant to continue forever. In other words, we are not meant to live permanently in the puʻuhonua. As explored in the introduction, puʻuhonua were places of refuge, places for rehabilitation, places to go and find safety before eventually returning to life outside of the sanctuary. At Puʻu Huluhulu, the hope is that people will someday (hopefully soon) not have to be there day after day because our mauna will be safe and our continued presence there no longer needed. The hope is that the land there can be left to rest and that people can go back to their homes and families. The hope is that the puʻuhonua continue to exist as a space of prayer and ceremony that doesn't need any physical structures to mark it. In other words, when Mauna Kea is safe and the TMT is disappeared from any and all dreams for the future, the tents will come down, the cars will be driven down the mountain, and the people will return home. What will remain, however, are the memories, the stories, and, perhaps most significantly, the pride, strength, and resilience imprinted on our hearts and souls. What will remain, additionally, is the knowledge that nothing can take away our experiences of the puʻuhonua (no matter where we experienced it from).

Kahiki as Sanctuary

Toward the beginning of this chapter, I reviewed a Kanaka orientation in the world through studying Kahikikū and Kahikimoe. Whenever I look at the horizon, from wherever I happen to be in the world, I understand myself in relation to them. Whether I am at Puʻu Huluhulu at the base of Mauna Kea, standing at the summit in ceremony, or across the ocean in Aotearoa, I know that as long as I exist in the pōʻai, or the circle, these Kahiki create for me, I am at the center of my own world, in control of the dreams that I create in it. What brings me strength and resolve in the midst of so much pain and devastation around the planet is the knowledge that Kahiki can never be taken from me. While colonial powers continue to encroach and attempt to strip us of our lands, stomping on our souls, I know that Kahiki is my ultimate sanctuary, my ultimate Indigenous space and time. It is where I can always go to find perspective. It is where I can always go to find refuge. It is where I can always go to dream. It has no limits. It is not bounded. Therefore, I can be free in it. When Puʻuhonua o Puʻuhuluhulu becomes a space without physical structures and returns to being a landscape of memories and meaning, I will use Kahiki and my knowledge of how to navigate nonphysical spaces and times to continually revisit it. Since the settler state relies upon taking and marking spaces, it will never try to steal Kahiki. It can't. It can't even exist there. Therefore, it will always be ours to visit, to shape, to use, and to share.

When I first learned about Kahiki as a little girl, dancing the stories of Moʻikeha and chanting the journeys of my great migrating ancestors, I truly had no idea what it would come to mean in my life. When I embarked on a new research journey to understand Kahiki in different ways, my appreciation for the brilliance of my ancestors grew. When I wrote my PhD thesis, I was amazed at how so much meaning could be packed into one word. I was inspired by the ways Kānaka worked with Kahiki, always using it to make sense of whatever was most pressing in their lives, whether it was their initial migrations to Hawaiʻi, their first interactions with European explorers, the colonial ambitions of the United States, or even the rehabilitation of Pacific connections in a new age of renaissance and cultural revival. When I began revising my thesis, wanting to turn it into a book, I realized that I could not simply publish what I wrote *then* because my confidence in Kahiki as a central concept for life had deepened and grown. My ideas about it had changed, just as it had for my kūpuna. Therefore, I sought to give it new function so that, as the title of this book implies, it can be ancient as it is constantly made new for the future. May we all be inspired to do the same, with our own concepts, at our own times, in our own spaces, always.

I Kahiki nō ke ola. In Kahiki there is life. Ola.

Notes

Preface

1. Angelou, "Our Grandmothers," 217.

Introduction

Epigraph. Lorde, *Sister Outsider*, 37.

1. In supporting movements to not make one's native tongue appear foreign, all text appearing in Hawaiian will not be italicized.
2. While it is not the goal of this book to cover the entire issue extensively, as that could be a book on its own, I want to acknowledge the great amount of literature that has already been produced about the mauna, particularly by other Kanaka Maoli scholars who have stood (and who continue to stand) for the protection of Mauna Kea. Among some of the authors who have written about the issue are Goodyear-Kaʻōpua, "Protectors of the Future"; Goodyear-Kaʻōpua and Mahelona, "Protecting Maunakea"; Maile, "Science, Time, and Mauna a Wākea," May 13, 2015; Maile, "Science, Time, and Mauna a Wākea," May 20, 2015; Maile, "For Mauna Kea to Live, TMT Must Leave"; Kuwada, "We Are Not Warriors"; Kuwada, "We Live in the Future"; Meyer, "Canoe, Wind, and Mountain"; Tengan, "Ka

Ulu Koa Ma Kai"; Kauanui, "Forum 2"; Casumbal-Salazar, "In Ceremony and Struggle"; and Silva, "Ke Mau Nei Nō Ke Ea"; among others.

3. Brestovansky, "Dozens of Kupuna Arrested."

4. The terms "Kanaka Maoli" and "Kanaka" will be used interchangably with "Hawaiian." When used to refer to more than one person, the plural forms "Kānaka Maoli" and "Kānaka" will be used.

5. Quite broadly, I use "Indigenous" to refer to the first peoples of a particular location. The politics and problematics of this term, however, will be explored throughout this book.

6. Teaiwa, "Asia-Pacific Studies Agenda," 116.

7. The phrase "our sea of islands" was popularized by Epeli Hau'ofa in an essay by the same name. His essay continues to be a critical work in Pacific studies. Hau'ofa, "Our Sea of Islands."

8. Valeri, *Kingship and Sacrifice*, 9.

9. Dening, "Sea People of the West," 289.

10. Adds, "E Kore Au e Ngaro," 17.

11. Greg Dening argues that Pulotu is a homeland located somewhere west of the Fijian Islands, a location from which some of the first Polynesians in the west would have migrated. Hawaiki, he explains, comprises the lands of Sāmoa, Tonga, and Fiji, a general area in the Pacific from which Polynesians in the east would have migrated. Hawaiki is also a central concept in Aotearoa, where Māori have many oral traditions recounting their connection to this homeland. Like Kahiki, however, it does not have a specific location but is more of a concept of origin and connection. Dening, "Sea People of the West," 289.

12. Cook, *Return to Kahiki*, 2–3.

13. Pukui, *'Ōlelo No'eau*, 9.

14. Chang, *World*, viii.

15. Both Noenoe Silva and Puakea Nogelmeier cite the work of prominent Kanaka Maoli scholar Samuel Kamakau, who presents a genealogy of travel and migration *before* Cook's arrival, thus rendering his coming to the islands far less remarkable than many Western historical sources have made it seem. Silva, *Aloha Betrayed*, 20; Nogelmeier, *Mai Pa'a i Ka Leo*, 135; Kamakau, "Ka Moolelo o Kamehameha I (Helu 7 [8])."

16. Cook, *Return to Kahiki*, 6–7.

17. Works by Pohnpeian poet Emelihter Kihleng and Marshallese poet Kathy Jetnil-Kijiner speak directly to this racial tension in Hawai'i. Kihleng, "Micronesian Question"; Jetnil-Kijiner, "Lessons from Hawai'i."

18. Pu'u Huluhulu is a hill located along the Saddle Road (now called the Daniel K. Inouye Highway) on the Big Island of Hawai'i.

19. HULI, "Kia'i of Maunakea."

20. Ibid.

21. The Māori Land March began on September 13, 1975, and was a thousand-kilometer march from Te Hāpua in the far north all the way to Wellington at the southern tip of the North Island. The march, which concluded on October 13, 1975, in Wellington, protested land alienation in Aotearoa. At the head of the

march was the seventy-nine-year-old Whina Cooper. The slogan for the march was "Not one more acre of Māori land."

22. Kamakau, "Ka Moolelo Hawaii (Helu 21)," 1.
23. Minerbi, "Sanctuaries," 116.
24. Tengan, *Native Men Remade*, 53.
25. Pukui and Elbert, *Hawaiian Dictionary*, 21.
26. Goodyear-Kaʻōpua, *Seeds We Planted*, 32; Kikiloi, "Rebirth of an Archipelago," 75; Silva, "I Kū Mau Mau," 18.
27. Kikiloi, "Rebirth of an Archipelago," 75.
28. Goodyear-Kaʻōpua, *Seeds We Planted*, 32.
29. This interpretation is supported by renowned Hawaiian scholar Mary Kawena Pukui and anthropologist E. S. Craighill Handy. They argue that ʻāina speaks to the act of "feeding": "The term ʻaina represented a concept essentially belonging to an agricultural people, deriving as it did from the verb ʻai, to feed, with the substantive suffix na added, so that it signified 'that which feeds' or 'feeder.'" Pukui and Handy, *Polynesian Family System*, 3.
30. Blaisdell, "I Hea Nā Kānaka Maoli?," 10.
31. Meyer, *Hoʻoulu*, 101.
32. Anderson, *Imagined Communities*, 6–7.
33. Ibid., 6.
34. Chandler, "On Being Indigenous," 86.
35. Osorio, "On Being Hawaiian," 23.
36. Hauʻofa, "Ocean in Us," 393.
37. Teaiwa, "Asia-Pacific Studies Agenda," 115.
38. Hauʻofa, "Ocean in Us," 393.
39. P. Kanahele, "I Am This Land," 25.

Chapter 1: The Edge

1. An official "Mauna Alert" was put out by leaders of Puʻuhonua o Puʻuhuluhulu on September 6, 2019, stating that they expected law enforcement action as early as dawn on Monday, September, 9, 2019. This alert was put out on social media, on Facebook and Instagram, calling for kiaʻi to come to the mauna.
2. Klein, *This Changes Everything*, 342.
3. Case, "Love of Place."
4. Tuan, *Topophilia*, 4.
5. Kelley, *Freedom Dreams*, 9.
6. On September 13, 2019, VicRoads (the roads authority of Victoria, Australia) workers arrived to begin cutting down trees. Some large branches were cut before a temporary halt was put on cutting any more. Hall, "Temporary Reprieve."
7. Mitchell, *Sacred Instructions*, 6.
8. McDougall, *Finding Meaning*, 118.
9. P. Kanahele, "I Am This Land, and This Land Is Me."
10. Stephenson, "On Being 'Close to Nature,'" 20.
11. Klein, *This Changes Everything*.

12. Stephenson, "On Being 'Close to Nature,'" 21.
13. Howkins, "Appropriating Space," 32–33.
14. Sissons, *First Peoples*, 17.
15. Purakayastha, "Eco-Incarceration," 256.
16. Carter, "Iwi," 31.
17. Ibid.
18. Wendt, "Towards a New Oceania"; Hau'ofa, "The Ocean in Us."
19. Emerging work by Emma Powell explores the Cook Islands concept of 'akapapa'anga. Rather than defining it as "genealogy," she describes it as a "social-cultural network that is organic, non-linear and perpetually growing." Her work challenges the equation of terms such as "mo'okū'auhau" and "'akapapa'anga" with the English "genealogy." Powell, "Te 'Akapapa Nei Tātou"; Pukui and Handy, *Polynesian Family System*, 197.
20. Chang, "Transcending Settler Colonial Boundaries," 96.
21. Ibid.
22. Wilson-Hokowhitu, "He Pukoa Kani 'āina," 141; Young, *Rethinking the Native Hawaiian Past*, 30–31.
23. Peralto, "Mauna a Wākea," 233–234.
24. Te Punga Somerville, *Once Were Pacific*, xxi.
25. James Clifford explains that the phrase "roots and routes" comes from diaspora discourse and speaks to the forming of "community consciousness and solidarity" in new homes away from home. Clifford, "Diasporas," 308. Margaret Jolly says, quite simply, that the phrase speaks to the tension between "movement and settlement." Jolly, "On the Edge?," 419.
26. H.-K. Trask, "Birth of the Modern Hawaiian Movement," 126.
27. Adds, "E Kore Au e Ngaro," 26.
28. Thiong'o, *Decolonising the Mind*, 3.
29. Carter, "Iwi."
30. Although modern orthography includes the use of the 'okina, or glottal stop, and the kahakō, or macron, most texts that come from the Hawaiian language newspapers do not. Therefore, quotations from these texts will be presented without these markings. My own writing, however, will use these diacritical marks to aid in pronunciation and interpretation.
31. In this chant, it is quite possible that Kahiki refers to Tahiti, especially considering that Poepoe uses the name "Tahiti" in his narrative. Abraham Fornander also uses "Tahiti." Fornander, *Account of the Polynesian Race*, 9–10. In his research, Ben Finney uses "Kahiki." Finney, "Myth."
32. In other versions, this is "mo'opuna" (grandchild) instead of "mokupuni" (island).
33. Poepoe, "Ka Moolelo Hawaii Kahiko," February 2, 1906, 1.
34. Unless otherwise indicated, all translations are my own.
35. Beckwith, *Hawaiian Mythology*, 359–360; Fornander, *Fornander Collection of Hawaiian Antiquities*, 6:253.
36. Chang, *World*, 14.
37. Ibid., 19.
38. Beckwith, *Hawaiian Mythology*, 309; McKinzie, *Hawaiian Genealogies:*, 2:5.
39. Poepoe, "Ka Moolelo Hawaii Kahiko," February 7, 1906, 1.

40. McDougall, *Finding Meaning*, 87.
41. Kamakau, "Ka Moolelo o Kamehameha I (Helu 7 [8])," 1.
42. Another important figure in Hawaiian moʻokūʻauhau is Pele, the volcano deity who dwells at Kīlauea on the Big Island of Hawaiʻi. In her book, kuʻualoha hoʻomanawanui cites chants and narratives of Pele's coming from Kahiki. In this case, she is said to come from Polapola, a specific place in Kahiki. Thus, like Papa, she too is not from Hawaiʻi. hoʻomanwanui, *Voices of Fire*.
43. Case, "Caught in the Currents."
44. M. N. Huang, "Ecologies of Entanglement," 95.
45. Republic of the Marshall Islands, "Tile Til Eo" 6.
46. State of Hawaiʻi Department of the Attorney General, "Final Report."
47. Aguon, *What We Bury at Night*, 19.
48. bid., 27–39.
49. Emelihter Kihleng's poem "The Micronesian Question" problematizes the term "Micronesian" by acknowleding the many different island groups and languages that it flattens. Kihleng, "The Micronesian Question"; Hofschneider, "Talking about Anti-Micronesian Hate."
50. Keanu Sai is one of the leading scholars who has proven the illegality of the takeover of Hawaiʻi. Sai, "American Occupation"; McDermott and Andrade, *People and Cultures of Hawaiʻi*, xv.
51. Kali Fermantez has argued that all Hawaiians have, at some point, been "dissed": "disrespected, disenfranchised, and dissconnected." Fermantez, "Re-Placing Hawaiians," 98.
52. Ritte quoted in Osorio, "Hawaiian Souls," 144.
53. Mitchell, *Sacred Instructions*, 46.

Chapter 2: Indigenous Crossings

1. Elmslie and Webb-Gannon, "Slow-Motion Genocide."
2. Said, *Representations of the Intellectual*, 11.
3. Ibid.
4. Cabrera, Matias, and Montoya, "Activism or Slactivism?," 400.
5. Christensen, "Political Activities on the Internet."
6. Qolouvaki, "Mana of Wansolwara."
7. LaDuke, *Militarization of Indian Country*, xii.
8. See Case, "Stories."
9. Goodyear-Kaʻōpua, *Seeds We Planted*, 189.
10. Noenoe Silva has written about how the decline of the Hawaiian language resulted in an inability to access works written in Hawaiian, and as a result, the knowledge of our ancestors as intellectuals. Silva, "E Lawe i Ke ō," 238.
11. Cook, *Return to Kahiki*, 3.
12. Kamakau, "Ka Moolelo o Kamehameha I (Helu 7 [8])," 1.
13. Nakaa, "He Moolelo Hawaii," 1.
14. Finney, "Myth," 387.
15. Nakaa, "He Moolelo Hawaii," 1.
16. Kuokoa, "Na Wanana," 3.

17. Cook, *Return to Kahiki*, 3.
18. Kuokoa, "Na Wanana," 3.
19. Silva, *Aloha Betrayed*, 80.
20. Hau'ofa, "Our Sea of Islands," 151.
21. Hau'ofa, "Ocean in Us," 392.
22. Ibid., 401.
23. Meyer, "Holographic Epistemology," 98.
24. Pukui and Elbert, *Hawaiian Dictionary*, 69.
25. Alfred, "Warrior Scholarship," 98.
26. Hau'ofa, "Ocean in Us"; Banivanua-Mar, *Decolonisation and the Pacific*.
27. Ibid., 2.
28. Macpherson, "Empowering Pacific Peoples."
29. Tracey Banivanua-Mar calls West Papua "an as yet poorly recognized site of settler-colonial violence against indigenous peoples" and identifies various settler colonial logics at work in the region. Banivanua-Mar, "Thousand Miles of Cannibal Lands," 583; Kauanui, "Forum 2."
30. Haimona-Riki, "Māori Visit Mauna Kea."
31. Allen, *Trans-Indigenous*.
32. Ibid., xiv.
33. Ibid.
34. Aikau, Goodyear-Ka'ōpua, and Silva, "Practice of Kuleana," 158.
35. RNZ, "World's Indigenous People Gather."
36. Martínez Cobo, "Study," 29.
37. United Nations, "United Nations Declaration," 7.
38. Banivanua-Mar, "Thousand Miles of Cannibal Lands," 585.
39. Chandler, "On Being Indigenous," 86.
40. L. T. Smith, *Decolonizing Methodologies*, 7.
41. Marinaccio, "We're Not Indigenous," 11.
42. Ibid., 8.
43. Chandler, "On Being Indigenous," 84.
44. H. Huang, "Review," 81–82.
45. H.-K. Trask, *From a Native Daughter*, 144.
46. Hau'ofa, "Our Sea of Islands," 153.
47. Kabutaulaka, "Re-Presenting Melanesia," 110.
48. Webb and Webb-Gannon, "Musical Melanesianism."
49. RNZ, "Pacific Scholars."
50. Gray quoted in Rovoi, "Renaming Oceania."

Chapter 3: What Is Below Shall Rise

1. It is estimated that over five thousand people, Hawaiians and non-Hawaiians, marched that day. M. B. Trask, "Hawaiian Sovereignty."
2. Chandler, "On Being Indigenous,'" 86.
3. La'anui, "He Manao Hoakaka Wale," 83.
4. Some accounts say he set out in 1812. Poepoe, "He Moolelo No Kamehameha I," 1.

5. "Peʻahi" can mean "to fan," "to beckon," "to wave," or "to signal." My translation represents what I hope to be the most broad interpretation of the phrase "peahi aku ka peahi" so as not to lock it into anything too specific. Laʻanui, "He Manao Hoakaka Wale," 83.
6. Charlot, "Note," 376.
7. Ibid.
8. Harjo, Spiral to the Stars, 5.
9. Lear, Radical Hope, 103.
10. Thiongʻo, Decolonising the Mind, 3.
11. Harjo, Spiral to the Stars, 50.
12. Recollect, "Gesturing Indigenous Futurities," 91.
13. Harjo, Spiral to the Stars, 4.
14. Laʻanui, "He Manao Hoakaka Wale."
15. Kamakau, "Ka Moolelo Hawaii (Helu 21)," 1.
16. "Ka Moolelo o Kamehameha I (Helu 44)," 1.
17. Kameʻeleihiwa, Native Land and Foreign Desires, 80.
18. Ibid., 68.
19. Teaiwa and Moekaʻa, "Comparative History in Polynesia."
20. Case, "Bringing the Pacific to Us," 17.
21. Lear, Radical Hope, 10.
22. This may either be a typo or an alternate spelling of the more common Milu.
23. S, "He Wanana," 31.
24. Charlot, "Note," 377.
25. Pukui, Haertig, and Lee, Nānā i Ke Kumu, 2:300.
26. Salesa, "When the Waters Met," 147.
27. Kauakoʻiawe, "Ke Kaao No Kapihe," 1.
28. Finney, "Sin at Awarua."
29. Valeri, Kingship and Sacrifice, 8.
30. Pukui and Elbert, Hawaiian Dictionary, 112; Tregear, Māori-Polynesian Comparative Dictionary, 499.
31. Kauakoʻiawe, "Ke Kaao No Kapihe," 1.
32. Hofmeyr, Gandhi's Printing Press, 7.
33. Nā Kiaʻi o ka Pō, "Na Wanana i Hooko Ia."
34. Ibid., 1.
35. "Peasant commoner" is a reference to Sanford B. Dole. Nā Kiaʻi o ka Pō, "Na Wanana i Hooko Ia," 1.
36. Ibid.
37. Silva, Aloha Betrayed, 80.
38. Cook, "Kahiki," 38.
39. Nā Kiaʻi o ke Ao, "Ahea La Pau Ke Kuhihewa o Ka Lahui," 3.
40. Ibid.
41. Nā Kiaʻi o ke Ao, "Ahea La Pau Ke Kuhihewa o Ka Lahui (Helu 2)," 1.
42. Kauakoʻiawe, "Ke Kaao No Kapihe," 1.
43. Hauʻofa, "Pasts to Remember," 61.
44. Harjo, Spiral to the Stars, 4.

45. Noenoe Silva's work has been critical in educating people about Kānaka Maoli resistance, particularly in regard to the 1897 petitions against US annexation. I have found the signatures of my great grandmother, Emma Paʻa, and my grandmother, Keala Hussey, in these petitions. Silva, *Aloha Betrayed*. Ray Kinney, my great-grandfather, had a half brother, William Ansel Kinney, who was a politician and prominent lobbyist for annexation.
46. Goodyear-Kaʻōpua, "Protectors of the Future," 185.
47. Hauʻofa, "Ocean in Us," 393.
48. Kauakoʻiawe, "Ke Kaao No Kapihe," 1.
49. Kuwada, "We Live in the Future."
50. Aikau, "Following the Alaloa Kīpapa," 659.

Chapter 4: Everything Ancient Was Once New

1. Big Island Video News, "Kanuha Arrest."
2. Brestovansky and Burnett, "Construction of TMT Authorized."
3. Ibid.
4. Teves, *Defiant Indigeneity*, 5.
5. G. Kanahele, *Hawaiian Renaissance*, 1.
6. Big Island Video News, "Kalepa Baybayan."
7. Debates about cultural construction, tradition, and authenticity between anthropologists Roger Keesing, Richard Handler, and Jocelyn Linnekin and Kānaka Maoli scholar Haunani-Kay Trask have been well documented and written about critically by Jeffrey Tobin, who examines the debates in the context of Hawaiian Nationalism. Keesing, "Culture and History"; Keesing, "Reply to Trask." Handler and Linnekin, "Tradition"; Linnekin, "Defining Tradition"; Linnekin, "Cultural Invention." H.-K. Trask, "Natives and Anthropologists." Tobin, "Cultural Construction."
8. Finney, "Myth"; Finney, "Sin at Awarua"; Finney, "Renaissance."
9. Finney, "Renaissance," 299.
10. Dening, "Endeavour and Hokuleʻa," 118.
11. Diaz, "Voyaging"; Hauʻofa, "Our Sea of Islands."
12. For more on the voyage, see Finney, *Hokuleʻa*; and Low, *Hawaiki Rising*.
13. Having grown up around many of these men, I refer to them affectionately as "Uncle."
14. Koa, or Acacia koa, is a large forest tree endemic to Hawaiʻi.
15. Bertelmann, interview with author.
16. Ibid.
17. Ty P. Kāwika Tengan's book is important in establishing the context within which (and after which) the movement to build *Mauloa* occured. Tengan, *Native Men Remade*.
18. "Voyage of Rediscovery" was the name given to an actual voyage that took place from 1985 to 1987 in which *Hōkūleʻa* journeyed to Aotearoa and back. During this voyage the canoe also made stops in Tahiti, the Cook Islands, Tonga, American Sāmoa, and the Tuamotu Islands. Kahapeʻa-Tanner, "Sailing the Ancestral Bridges," 177.

19. I've previously published on the process of interviewing the canoe builders. Case, "Pehea Ka ʻAha a Kāua?"
20. Lear, *Radical Hope*, 36.
21. Ibid., 37.
22. Bertelmann interview.
23. At time of writing, Nā Kālai Waʻa, the organization responsible for the building and maintenance of *Mauloa* and the double-hulled canoe *Makaliʻi*, is working to restore *Mauloa*.
24. Grace, interview with author.
25. Chandler, "On Being Indigenous," 84.
26. Harjo, *Spiral to the Stars*, 5.
27. Chandler, "On Being Indigenous."
28. Goodyear-Kaʻōpua, *Seeds We Planted*, 8.
29. Kanuha's words were transcribed directly from a filmed interview. I have chosen to maintain his exact words and not correct them for grammar.
30. Big Island Video News, "Kanuha Arrest."
31. Ludlow et al., "Double Binds," 54.
32. Teves, *Defiant Indigeneity*, 6.
33. Narayan, "How Native Is a 'Native'?," 676.
34. Ibid.
35. For critiques of the term "traditional," see Mallon, "Against Tradition"; and Wendt, "Towards a New Oceania."
36. Many of the kālai waʻa interviewed used Pidgin, also known as Hawaiʻi Creole English. Rather than correcting their grammar to make their words appear "correct" in English, I've chosen to maintain their voice, and in doing so, honor the importance of Pidgin as an identity marker in Hawaiʻi. This choice also reflects my insistence that Pidgin not be regarded as a "broken" or lesser version of English but as a complex vernacular with its own history and meaning.
37. Grace interview.
38. Pilago, interview with author.
39. Wendt, "Towards a New Oceania," 76.
40. This translation is by the editor of *He Lei No ʻEmalani*. Nogelmeier, *He Lei No ʻEmalani*, 268.

Chapter 5: To the Bones

1. Newcomb, *Pagans in the Promised Land*, 91.
2. Deloria, "Conquest Masquerading as Law," 96.
3. Ibid.
4. Harry, "Might Makes Right."
5. Events kicked off in October and ended in December 2019.
6. In Aotearoa, "Pacific" is often used to refer to people from the seven largest Pacific ethnic groups in the country: Samoan, Tongan, Tokelauan, Cook Islands Māori, Fijian, Niuean, and Tuvaluan.
7. In this chapter, I am considering Aotearoa as part of the Pacific. This is important because the distinction between tangata whenua and other Pacific peoples,

while relevant in many contexts, has led to ambivalence about whether or not Māori are in fact Pacifc Islanders. Alice Te Punga Somerville has written more extensively about this in her book. Te Punga Somerville, *Once Were Pacific: Māori Connections to Oceania.*

8. TVNZ, "Movement to Boycott."

9. Suzanne Tamaki, an artist based in Wellington, gathered 250 artists to create anti-Cook exhibitions around the country. McLachlan, "Critics."

10. Alice Te Punga Somerville's essay identifies some of the many different ways Cook has affected the region. Te Punga Somerville, "Two Hundred and Fifty Ways."

11. In early 2019, "One Treaty, One Nation" pamphlets were distributed to letterboxes in Point Chevalier, Auckland. They pushed the idea that there should be "no special representation of part-Maoris in local government" and that New Zealand should "end the stranglehold that one minority group has over the culture and life of the nation." The pamphlets also argued that the benefits brought to Māori by colonization outweighed the consequences. Academics called them "anti-Māori" and examples of "hate speech." Woolf and Loren, "One Treaty, One Nation Pamphlet."

12. Cavanagh, "History," 39.

13. Veracini, "On Settlerness," 1.

14. Kauanui and Wolfe, "Settler Colonialism," 239.

15. Ibid., 237.

16. Byrd, *Transit of Empire.*

17. Byrd, *Transit of Empire*, xix.

18. Rohrer, *Staking Claim*, 62.

19. Ibid., 70.

20. Byrd, *Transit of Empire*, xxxviii–xxxiv.

21. Justice, "Better World Becoming," 27.

22. Smith argues that the place name Aotearoa/New Zealand "literally demonstrates the settler/native divide" and promotes the notion of biculturalism. J. Smith, "Post-Cultural Hospitality," 68. Ibid., 84.

23. Though I have chosen to use the term "settler colonialism" in my writing, I also recognize that some Indigenous scholars find it problematic. At a talk about the Doctrine of Discovery held in September 2019, Moana Jackson challeneged my use of the term, arguing that "settle" is a calming term that actually divorces colonizers from the unsettling they cause in their colonial conquests. While understanding his concerns and reflecting on his challenge to think of new terms, my choice to use it comes from my wanting to align this work with the wealth of literature already published on settler colonialism and to position this work among the many robust and ongoing conversations about it.

24. Wolfe, "Settler Colonialism," 388.

25. Ibid., 387.

26. Rowse, "Indigenous Heterogeneity," 301.

27. Johnson, "Writing Indigenous Histories," 317; Rowse, "Indigenous Heterogeneity," 301.

28. Howkins, "Appropriating Space," 49.

29. Ibid.

30. Manatū Taonga Ministry for Culture and Heritage, "Naming Tuia—Encounters 250?"
31. Murphyao and Black, "Unsettling Settler Belonging," 317.
32. Byrnes, "Dead Sheet," 24.
33. Manatū Taonga Ministry for Culture and Heritage, "About Tuia 250."
34. Cavanagh, "History," 17–18.
35. Ranford, "Human Rights Advocate."
36. There were Māori who chose to participate in the events. In May 2019, the names of the vessels that would participate in the Tuia 250 Voyage were announced. Among the vessels included were two waka hourua (double-hulled canoes), *Haunui* from Tāmaki Makaurau (Auckland), and *Ngahiraka Mai Tawhiti* from Tauranga. From October to December 2019, these canoes joind a replica of Cook's *Endeavour* and sailed to various sites around Aotearoa. Manatū Taonga Ministry for Culture and Heritage, "Tuia 250 Voyage Flotilla Announced."
37. Ngata, "Why I Won't."
38. Ibid.
39. Jackson, "James Cook." Kahukiwa founded a Facebook group called Kia Mau where Indigenous peoples could sign a declaration of nonparticipation in Tuia 250 events.
40. The Captain Cook statue on Titirangi (also known as Kaiti Hill) in Gisborne has been the target of ongoing defacement for the past few years. Cooke, "Captain Cook Statue." On May 3, 2019, it was relocated to the Tairāwhiti Museum. Desmarais, "Captain Cook." Jackson, "James Cook."
41. Howe, "Review," 108.
42. Some believe Hawaiians thought Captain Cook was their god, Lono, arriving during the time of Makahiki, a time of peace when Lono reigned.
43. Howe, "Review"; Sahlins, *How "Natives" Think*; Obeyesekere, *Apotheosis of Captain Cook*.
44. Ellis, *Journal of William Ellis*, 52.
45. Beaglehole, *Life of Captain James Cook*, 676.
46. Byrd, *Transit of Empire*, 125.
47. Rohrer, *Staking Claim*, 12.
48. Ibid.
49. Ibid., 14.

Chapter 6: In Kahiki There Is Life

1. Kelley, *Freedom Dreams*, 7.
2. Rifkin, *Beyond Settler Time*, 3.
3. Callis, "Kim Finalizing Maunakea Committee."
4. Ibid.
5. Ibid.
6. Ibid.
7. Ibid.
8. Rifkin, *Beyond Settler Time*, 1.
9. Poepoe, "Moolelo Hawaii Kahiko," June 21, 1906, 1.

10. Keʻāpapanuʻu may be another name for Kahiki-ka-papa-nuʻu, or the layer of the atmosphere above Kahikikū. In other versions of this chant, this line is then followed by "Hānau Keʻāpapalani," which could be another name for Kahiki-ka-papa-lani, the layer of the atmosphere above Keʻāpapanuʻu. Poepoe's version, for some reason, does not include this line. In some versions, above Kahiki-ka-papa-nuʻu is Kahiki-kapu-i-Hōlani-ke-kuʻina. There are other variants of these names, including Kahikiikeʻāpapanuʻu and Kahikiikeʻāpapalani. Malo, "Ka Moʻolelo Hawaiʻi," 12; Pukui and Elbert, *Hawaiian Dictionary*, 112. Manu, "He Moolelo Kaao No Keaomelemele [Helu 1]," 1.
11. Malo, "Ka Moʻolelo Hawaiʻi," 12.
12. Ibid.
13. Pukui and Elbert, *Hawaiian Dictionary*, 112.
14. "Moolelo Hawaii Kahiko," June 26, 1906.
15. The two suffixes "kū" and "moe" mean "to stand" and "to sleep or to lie down," respectively.
16. Valeri, *Kingship and Sacrifice*, 9.
17. Kikiloi, "Rebirth of an Archipelago," 87.
18. Valeri, *Kingship and Sacrifice*, 8.
19. Ibid.
20. Rifkin, *Beyond Settler Time*, 2.
21. Ibid., 2–3.
22. Oliveira, *Ancestral Places*, 48.
23. It should be noted that kiaʻi have taken advantage of all different platforms on social media to share stories, insights, opinions, and information not covered by the mainstream media.
24. AP News, "Big Island 'Peace Park' Plan."
25. Ibid.
26. Banivanua-Mar, "Carving Wilderness," 76.
27. Ibid., 87.
28. Naʻputi and Bevacqua, "Militarization and Resistance," 846–847.
29. Hornung, *U.S. Military Laydown*, 27.
30. Santos Perez, "Blue-Washing."
31. A military buildup was first proposed in 2006 in response to tensions on other military bases in Okinawa. The plan is to relocate "as many as eight thousand US Marines from Okinana with their nine thousand dependents . . . more than doubling the size of the current US military presence on Guåhan." Naʻputi and Bevacqua, "Militarization and Resistance," 845, 847.
32. Callis, "Kim Finalizing Maunakea Committee."
33. Moreton-Robinson, *White Possessive*, xi.
34. Ibid., xiii.
35. Niheu, "Puʻuhonua," 164.
36. Ibid., 165.
37. Meyer, "Canoe, Wind, and Mountain," 132.
38. Harjo, *Spiral to the Stars*, 10.

Bibliography

Adds, Peter. "E Kore Au e Ngaro: Ancestral Connections to the Pacific." In *Tangata o Le Moana: New Zealand and the People of the Pacific*, edited by Sean Mallon, Kolokesa Māhina-Tuai, and Damon Salesa, 17–36. Wellington: Te Papa Press, 2012.

Aguon, Julian. *What We Bury at Night: Disposable Humanity*. Tokyo: Blue Ocean Press, 2008.

Aikau, Hōkūlani. "Following the Alaloa Kīpapa of Our Ancestors: A Trans-Indigenous Futurity without the State (United States or Otherwise)." *American Quarterly* 67, no. 3 (2015): 653–661.

Aikau, Hōkūlani, Noelani Goodyear-Kaʻōpua, and Noenoe Silva. "The Practice of Kuleana: Reflections on Critical Indigenous Studies through Trans-Indigenous Exchanges." In *Critical Indigenous Studies: Engagements in First World Locations*, edited by Aileen Moreton-Robinson, 157–175. Tucson: University of Arizona Press, 2016.

Alfred, Taiaiake. "Warrior Scholarship: Seeing the University as a Ground of Contention." In *Indigenizing the Academy: Transforming Scholarship and Empowering Communities*, edited by Devon Abbott Mihesuah and Angela Cavender Wilson, 88–99. Lincoln: University of Nebraska Press, 2004.

Allen, Chadwick. *Trans-Indigenous: Methodologies for Global Native Literary Studies.* Minneapolis: University of Minnesota Press, 2012.

Anderson, Benedict. *Imagined Communities: Reflections on the Origin and Spread of Nationalism.* 2nd ed. London: Verso, 2006.

Angelou, Maya. "Our Grandmothers." *Essence* 26, no. 1 (1995): 216–217.

AP News. "Big Island 'Peace Park' Plan Opposed by Telescope Protesters." *AP News.* July 2, 2017. https://www.apnews.com.

Banivanua-Mar, Tracey. "Carving Wilderness: Queenslands's National Parks and the Unsettling of Emptied Lands, 1890–1910." In *Making Settler Colonial Space: Perspectives on Race, Place, and Identity,* edited by Tracey Banivanua-Mar and Penelope Edmonds, 73–94. Eastbourne, UK: Palgrave Macmillan, 2010.

———. *Decolonisation and the Pacific: Indigenous Globalisation and the Ends of Empire.* Cambridge: Cambridge University Press, 2016.

———. "'A Thousand Miles of Cannibal Lands': Imagining Away Genocide in the Re-Colonization of West Papua." *Journal of Genocide Research* 10, no. 4 (2008): 583–602.

Beaglehole, John Cawte. *The Life of Captain James Cook.* London: Adam & Charles Black, 1974.

Beckwith, Martha. *Hawaiian Mythology.* Honolulu: University of Hawai'i Press, 1970.

Bertelmann, Milton Shorty. Interview with the author, November 23, 2013, Waimea, Hawai'i.

Big Island Video News. "Kalepa Baybayan Slams TMT Moratorium Proposal." *Big Island Video News,* July 24, 2019. https://www.bigislandvideonews.com.

———. "Kanuha Arrest on Mauna Kea as Police Dismantle Ahu." *Big Island Video News.* June 20, 2019. https://www.bigislandvideonews.com.

Blaisdell, Kekuni. "I Hea Nā Kānaka Maoli? Whither the Hawaiians?" *Hūlili: Multidisciplinary Research on Hawaiian Well-Being* 2, no. 1 (2005): 9–18.

Brestovansky, Michael. "Dozens of Kupuna Arrested on Third Consecutive Day of TMT Protest." *Hawai'i Tribune Herald,* July 18, 2019. https://www.hawaiitribune-herald.com.

Brestovansky, Michael, and John Burnett. "Construction of TMT Authorized; Opponents Vow to 'Fight for Our Rights.'" *Hawai'i Tribune Herald,* August 26, 2019. https://www.hawaiitribune-herald.com.

Byrd, Jodi. *Transit of Empire: Indigenous Critiques of Colonialism.* Minneapolis: University of Minnesota Press, 2011.

Byrnes, Giselle. "'A Dead Sheet Covered with Meaningless Words?': Place Names and the Cultural Colonization of Tauranga." *New Zealand Journal of History* 36, no. 1 (2002): 18–35.

Cabrera, Nolan L., Cheryl E. Matias, and Roberto Montoya. "Activism or Slactivism? The Potential and Pitfalls of Social Media in Contemporary Student Activism." *Journal of Diversity in Higher Education* 10, no. 4 (2017): 400–415.

Callis, Tom. "Kim Finalizing Maunakea Committee: Mission Statement Emphasizes Native Hawaiians' Connection to the Mountain, Exploration." *Hawai'i Tribune Herald,* February 22, 2018. https://www.hawaiitribune-herald.com.

Carter, Lynette. "''Iwi, Are Where the People Are.' Re-Thinking Ahi Kā and Ahi Mātao in Contemporary Māori Society." In *Home: Here to Stay*, edited by Mere Kēpa, Marilyn McPherson, and Linitā Manuʻatu, 23–32. Wellington: Huia Publishers, 2015.

Case, Emalani. "Bringing the Pacific to Us: A Tribute to Teresia Teaiwa, 1968–2017." *Archifacts: Journal of the Archives and Records Association of New Zealand Te Huinga Mahara*, no. 2 (2018): 15–20.

———. "Caught (and Brought) in the Currents: Narratives of Convergence, Destruction, and Creation at Kamilo Beach." *Journal of Transnational American Studies* 10, no. 1 (2019): 73–92.

———. "I Kahiki Ke Ola, In Kahiki There Is Life: Ancestral Memories and Migrations in the New Pacific." PhD thesis, Victoria University of Wellington, 2015.

———. "Love of Place: Towards a Critical Pacific Studies Pedagogy." Paper presented at Association for Social Anthropology in Oceania Conference, Auckland, New Zealand, 2019.

———. "Pehea Ka ʻAha a Kāua? How Is Our Rope? Ethnographic Practices from behind, in front of, and in the ʻAha." In *Global South Ethnographies: Minding the Senses*, edited by elke emerald, Rinehart, Robert E., and Antonio Garcia, 113–124. Rotterdam, Netherlands: Sense Publishers, 2016.

———. "The Stories We Choose to Tell Ourselves about Ourselves." *He Wahī Paʻakai* (blog), July 9, 2018. https://hewahipaakai.wordpress.com.

Casumbal-Salazar, Iokepa. "In Ceremony and Struggle: The Lāhui at Puʻuhonua o Puʻuhuluhulu." *Abusable Past*, August 14, 2019. https://www.radicalhistoryreview .org.

Cavanagh, Edward. "History, Time and the Indigenist Critique." *Arena Journal*, no. 37/38 (2012): 16–39.

Chandler, Michael J. "On Being Indigenous: An Essay on the Hermeneutics of ʻCultural Identity.ʼ" *Human Development* 56, no. 2 (2013): 83–97.

Chang, David A. "Transcending Settler Colonial Boundaries with Moʻokūʻauhau: Genealogy as Transgressive Methodology." In *The Past before Us: Moʻokūʻauhau as Methodology*, edited by Nālani Wilson-Hokowhitu, 94–105. Honolulu: University of Hawaiʻi Press, 2019.

———. *The World and All the Things upon It: Native Hawaiian Geographies of Exploration*. Minneapolis: University of Minnesota Press, 2016.

Charlot, John. "A Note on the Hawaiian Prophecy of Kapihe." *Journal of Pacific History* 39, no. 3 (2004): 375–377.

Christensen, Henrik Serup. "Political Activities on the Internet: Slacktivism or Political Participation by Other Means?" *First Monday: Peer-Reviewed Journal on the Internet* 16, no. 2 (February 7, 2011). https://journals.uic.edu.

Clifford, James. "Diasporas." *Cultural Anthropology* 9, no. 3 (1994): 302–338.

Cook, Kealani. "Kahiki: Native Hawaiian Relationships with Other Pacific Islanders, 1850–1915." PhD diss., University of Michigan, 2011.

———. *Return to Kahiki: Native Hawaiians in Oceania*. Cambridge: Cambridge University Press, 2018.

Cooke, Henry. "Captain Cook Statue in Gisborne Repeatedly Defaced." *Stuff*, August 1, 2016. https://www.stuff.co.nz.

Deloria, Vine. "Conquest Masquerading as Law." In *Unlearning the Language of Conquest: Scholars Expose Anti-Indianism in America*, edited by Donald Trent Jacobs, 94–107. Texas: University of Texas Press, 2006.

Dening, Greg. "Endeavour and Hokuleʻa." In *Readings/Writings*, 100–119. Melbourne: Melbourne University Press, 1994.

———. "Sea People of the West." *Geographical Review* 97, no. 2 (2007): 288–301.

Desmarais, Felix. "Captain Cook Finally Going inside after 50 Years." *Stuff*, April 30, 2019. https://www.stuff.co.nz.

Diaz, Vicente. "Voyaging for Anti-Colonial Recovery: Austronesian Seafaring, Archipelagic Rethinking, and the Re-Mapping of Indigeneity." *Pacific Asia Inquiry* 2, no. 1 (2011): 21–32.

Ellis, Willam. *Journal of William Ellis: A Narrative of a Tour through Hawaii in 1823*. Honolulu: Mutual Publishing, 2004.

Elmslie, Jim, and Camellia Webb-Gannon. "A Slow-Motion Genocide: Indonesian Rule in West Papua." *Griffith Journal of Law and Human Dignity* 1, no. 2 (2013): 142–166.

Fermantez, Kali. "Re-Placing Hawaiians in Dis Place We Call Home." *Hūlili: Multidisciplinary Research on Hawaiian Well-Being* 8 (2012): 97–131.

Finney, Ben. *Hokuleʻa: The Way to Tahiti*. New York: Dodd, Mead, 1979.

———. "Myth, Experiment, and the Reinvention of Polynesian Voyaging." *American Anthropologist* 93, no. 2 (1991): 383–404.

———. "Renaissance." In *Vaka Moana, Voyages of the Ancestors: The Discovery and Settlement of the Pacific*, edited by K. Howe, 288–333. Honolulu: University of Hawaiʻi Press, 2006.

———. "The Sin at Awarua." *Contemporary Pacific* 11, no. 1 (1999): 1–33.

Fornander, Abraham. *An Account of the Polynesian Race: Its Origins and Migrations and the Ancient History of the Hawaiian People to the Times of Kamehameha I*. London: Trubner, Ludgate Hill, 1880.

———. *Fornander Collection of Hawaiian Antiquities and Folk-Lore: The Account of the Formation of Their Islands and Origin of Their Race with the Traditions of Their Migrations, Etc. as Gathered from Original Sources*. Vol. 6. Honolulu: Bishop Museum Press, 1920.

Goodyear-Kaʻōpua, Noelani. "Protectors of the Future, Not Protestors of the Past: Indigenous Pacific Activism and Mauna a Wākea." *South Atlantic Quarterly* 116, no. 1 (2017): 184–194.

———. *The Seeds We Planted: Portraits of a Native Hawaiian Charter School*. Minneapolis: University of Minnesota Press, 2013.

Goodyear-Kaʻōpua, Noelani, and Yvonne Mahelona. "Protecting Maunakea Is a Mission Grounded in Tradition." *Zora*, September 5, 2019. https://zora.mediu m.com.

Grace, Charlie. Interview with the author, February 11, 2014, Hōnaunau, Hawaiʻi.

Haimona-Riki, Mare. "Māori Visit Mauna Kea as Hawaiians Visit Ihumātao." *Te Ao Māori News*, August 8, 2019. https://teaomaori.news.

Hall, Bianca. "Temporary Reprieve for Ancient Djab Wurrung Trees." *Age*, September 13, 2019. https://www.theage.com.au.

Handler, Richard, and Jocelyn Linnekin. "Tradition, Genuine or Spurious." *Journal of American Folklore* 97, no. 385 (1984): 273–290.

Harjo, Laura. *Spiral to the Stars: Mvskoke Tools of Futurity.* Tucson: University of Arizona Press, 2019.

Harry, Debra. "Might Makes Right: Resisting the Legal Fictions Underlying the Doctrine of Discovery." Presented at the Native American and Indigenous Studies Association (NAISA), Waikato, New Zealand, July 27, 2019. https://www.youtube.com.

Hauʻofa, Epeli. "The Ocean in Us." *Contemporary Pacific* 10, no. 2 (1998): 391–410.

———. "Our Sea of Islands." *Contemporary Pacific* 6, no. 1 (1994): 147–161.

———. "Pasts to Remember." In *We Are the Ocean: Selected Works*, 60–79. Honolulu: University of Hawaiʻi Press, 2008.

Hofmeyr, Isabel. *Gandhi's Printing Press: Experiments in Slow Reading.* Cambridge, MA: Harvard University Press, 2013.

Hofschneider, Anita. "Why Talking about Anti-Micronesian Hate Is Important." *Civil Beat Honolulu*, September 24, 2018. https://www.civilbeat.org.

hoʻomanwanui, kuʻualoha. *Voices of Fire: Reweaving the Literary Lei of Pele and Hiʻiaka.* Minneapolis: University of Minnesota Press, 2014.

Hornung, Jeffrey. *The U.S. Military Laydown on Guam: Progress amid Challenges.* Washington, DC: Sasakawa Peace Foundation, 2017.

Howe, Kerry R. "Review: The Making of Cook's Death." *Journal of Pacific History* 31, no. 1 (1996): 108–118.

Howkins, Adrian. "Appropriating Space: Antarctic Imperialism and the Mentality of Settler Colonialism." In *Making Settler Colonial Space: Perspectives on Race, Place, and Identity*, edited by Tracey Banivanua-Mar and Penelope Edmonds, 29–52. Eastbourne, UK: Palgrave Macmillan, 2010.

Huang, Hsinya. "Review: Toward the Trans-Indigenous Pacific: Islanding Perspectives." *Verge: Studies in Global Asias* 4, no. 2 (2018): 81–86.

Huang, Michelle N. "Ecologies of Entanglement in the Great Pacific Garbage Patch." *Journal of Asian American Studies* 20, no. 1 (2017): 95–117.

HULI. "Kiaʻi of Maunakea and the Royal Order of Kamehameha Designate Puʻu Huluhulu as a Puʻuhonua for the Safety of the People." Facebook. HULI (Hawaiian Unity and Liberation Institute), July 12, 2019. https://www.facebook.com.

Jackson, Moana. "James Cook and Our Monuments to Colonisation." *E-Tangata* (blog), June 2, 2019. https://e-tangata.co.nz.

Jetnil-Kijiner, Kathy. "Lessons from Hawaiʻi." In *Iep Jāltok: Poems from a Marshallese Daughter*, 45–49. Tucson: University of Arizona Press, 2017.

Johnson, Miranda. "Writing Indigenous Histories." *Australian Historical Studies* 45, no. 3 (2014): 317–330.

Jolly, Margaret. "On the Edge?: Deserts, Oceans, Islands." *Contemporary Pacific* 13, no. 2 (2001): 417–466.

Justice, Daniel Heath. "A Better World Becoming: Placing Critical Indigenous Studies." In *Critical Indigenous Studies*, edited by Aileen Moreton-Robinson, 19–32. Tucson: University of Arizona Press, 2016.

Kabutaulaka, Tarcisius. "Re-Presenting Melanesia: Ignoble Savages and Melanesian Alter-Natives." *Contemporary Pacific* 27, no. 1 (2015): 110–146.

Kahapeʻa-Tanner, Bonnie. "Sailing the Ancestral Bridges of Oceanic Knowledge." In *The Value of Hawaiʻi 2: Ancestral Roots, Oceanic Visions*, edited by Aiko Yamashiro and Noelani Goodyear-Kaʻōpua, 173–180. Honolulu: University of Hawaiʻi Press, 2014.

Kamakau, Samuel. "Ka Moolelo Hawaii (Helu 21)." *Ke Au Okoa*. March 10, 1870, 47 edition.

———. "Ka Moolelo o Kamehameha I (Helu 7 [8])." *Ka Nupepa Kuokoa*. December 22, 1866.

———. "Ka Moolelo o Kamehameha I (Helu 44)." *Ka Nupepa Kuokoa*. October 5, 1867.

Kameʻeleihiwa, Lilikalā. *Native Land and Foreign Desires: Pehea Lā e Pono Ai?* Honolulu: Bishop Museum Press, 1992.

Kanahele, George. *Hawaiian Renaissance*. Honolulu: Project Waiaha, 1982.

Kanahele, Pualani. "I Am This Land, and This Land Is Me." *Hūlili: Multidisciplinary Research on Hawaiian Well-Being* 2, no. 1 (2005): 21–30.

Kauakoʻiawe, J. D. "Ke Kaao No Kapihe." *Ka Hoku o Ka Pakipika*. March 20, 1862.

Kauanui, J. Kēhaulani. "Forum 2 / Enduing Hawaiian Sovereignty: Protecting the Sacred at Mauna Kea, Introduction." *Abusable Past*, August 14, 2019. https://www.radicalhistoryreview.org.

Kauanui, J. Kēhaulani, and Patrick Wolfe. "Settler Colonialism Then and Now: A Conversation Between J. Kēhaulani Kauanui and Patrick Wolfe." *Politica & Societa* 1 (2012): 235–258.

Keesing, Roger. "Culture and History in the Pacific." *Current Anthropology* 28, no. 4 (1987): 565–565.

———. "Reply to Trask." *Contemporary Pacific* 3, no. 1 (1991): 145–177.

Kelley, Robin D. G. *Freedom Dreams: The Black Radical Imagination*. Boston: Beacon Press, 2002.

Kihleng, Emelihter. "The Micronesian Question." In *Indigenous Literatures from Micronesia*, edited by Evelyn Flores and Emelihter Kihleng, 183–187. Honolulu: University of Hawaiʻi Press, 2019.

Kikiloi, Kekuewa. "Rebirth of an Archipelago: Sustaining a Hawaiian Cultural Identity for People and Homeland." *Hūlili: Multidisciplinary Research on Hawaiian Well-Being* 6 (2010): 73–115.

Klein, Naomi. *This Changes Everything: Capitalism vs. the Climate*. London: Penguin Books, 2014.

Kuokoa. "Na Wanana o Ke Au i Hala." *Ka Nupepa Kuokoa*. April 15, 1893.

Kuwada, Bryan Kamaoli. "We Are Not Warriors. We Are a Grove of Trees." *Ke Kaupu Hehi Ale* (blog), July 6, 2015. https://hehiale.wordpress.com.

———. "We Live in the Future. Come Join Us." *Ke Kaupu Hehi Ale* (blog), April 3, 2015. https://hehiale.wordpress.com.

Laʻanui, Gideona. "He Manao Hoakaka Wale No Keia No Koʻu Hanau Ana, a Me Koʻu Kamalii Ana, a Me Koʻu Hookanaka Ana, a Me Ka Ike Ana i Kekahi Mau Mea Oloko o Ke Aupuni o Kamehameha." *Ke Kumu Hawaii*. March 14, 1838.

LaDuke, Winona. *The Militarization of Indian Country*. East Lansing: Michigan State University Press, 2012.

Lear, Jonathan. *Radical Hope: Ethics in the Face of Cultural Devastation*. Cambridge, MA: Harvard University Press, 2006.

Linnekin, Jocelyn. "Cultural Invention and the Dilemma of Authenticity." *American Anthropologist* 93, no. 2 (1991): 446–449.

———. "Defining Tradition: Variations on the Hawaiian Identity." *American Ethnologist* 10, no. 2 (1983): 241–252.

Lorde, Audre. *Sister Outsider: Essays and Speeches by Audre Lorde.* Berkeley, CA: Crossing Press, 2007.

Low, Sam. *Hawaiki Rising: Hōkūleʻa, Nainoa Thompson, and the Hawaiian Renaissance.* Honolulu: Island Heritage Publishing, 2013.

Ludlow, Francis, Lauren Baker, Samara Brock, Chris Hebdon, and Michael R. Dove. "The Double Binds of Indigeneity and Indigenous Resistance." *Humanities* 5, no. 3 (2016): 53–71.

Macpherson, Cluny. "Empowering Pacific Peoples: Community Organisations in New Zealand." In *Tangata o Le Moana: New Zealand and the People of the Pacific,* edited by Sean Mallon, Kolokesa Māhina-Tuai, and Damon Salesa, 179–199. Wellington: Te Papa Press, 2012.

Maile, David. "For Mauna Kea to Live, TMT Must Leave." *Abusalble Past,* August 14, 2019. https://www.radicalhistoryreview.org.

———. "Science, Time, and Mauna a Wākea: The Thirty-Meter Telescope's Capitalist-Colonialist Violence, Part I." May 13, 2015. https://therednation.org.

———. "Science, Time, and Mauna a Wākea: The Thirty-Meter Telescope's Capitalist-Colonialist Violence, Part II." May 20, 2015. https://therednation.org.

Mallon, Sean. "Against Tradition." *Contemporary Pacific* 22, no. 2 (2010): 362–381.

Malo, David. "Ka Moʻolelo Hawaiʻi." Unpublished manuscript, 2008.

Manatū Taonga Ministry for Culture and Heritage. "About Tuia 250." *Tuia Encounters 250* (blog), February 12, 2019. https://www.tuia250.nz.

———. "Naming Tuia—Encounters 250?" *Tuia Encounters 250* (blog), January 21, 2019. https://www.tuia250.nz.

Manu, Mose. "He Moolelo Kaao No Keaomelemele [Helu 1]." *Nupepa Kuokoa.* September 6, 1884, 36 edition.

Marinaccio, Jess. "'We're Not Indigenous. We're Just, We're Us': Taiwan's Austronesian Diplomacy and Indigeneity in the Independent Pacific." Paper presented at the Native American and Indigenous Studies Association Conference, Waikato, New Zealand, 2019.

Martínez Cobo, José R. "Study of the Problem of Discrimination against Indigenous Populations." Vol. 5, "Conclusions, Proposals and Recommendations." New York: United Nations, 1987.

McDermott, John F., and Naleen Naupaka Andrade. *People and Cultures of Hawaiʻi: The Evolution of Culture and Ethnicity.* Hawaiʻi: University of Hawaiʻi Press, 2011.

McDougall, Brandy Nālani. *Finding Meaning: Kaona and Contemporary Hawaiian Literature.* Tucson: University of Arizona Press, 2016.

McKinzie, Edith Kawelohea. *Hawaiian Genealogies: Extracted from Hawaiian Language Newspapers.* Vol. 2. Honolulu: University of Hawaiʻi Press, 1997.

McLachlan, Leigh-Marama. "Critics Say the $20 Million Cook Landing Commemorations Ignore Māori Pain." *Spinoff* (blog), May 10, 2019. https://thespinoff.co.nz.

Meyer, Manulani Aluli. "The Canoe, the Wind, and the Mountain: Shunting the

'Rashomon Effect' of Mauna Kea: An Aloha Aina Response." *Pacific Studies* 41, no. 3 (2018): 131–133.

———. "Holographic Epistemology: Native Common Sense." *China Media Research* 9, no. 2 (2013): 94–101.

———. *Hoʻoulu: Our Time of Becoming: Hawaiian Epistemology and Early Writings*. Honolulu: ʻAi Pōhaku Press, 2003.

Minerbi, Luciano. "Sanctuaries, Places of Refuge, and Indigenous Knowledge in Hawaiʻi." In *Science of Pacific Island Peoples: Land Use and Agriculture*, edited by John Morrison, Paul Geraghty, and Linda Crowl, 89–129. Vol. 2. Suva: Institute of Pacific Studies, 1994.

Ministry for Culture and Heritage. "Tuia 250 Voyage Flotilla Announced." May 14, 2019. http://www.scoop.co.nz.

Mitchell, Sherri. *Sacred Instructions: Indigenous Wisdom for Living Spirit-Based Change*. Berkeley, CA: North Atlantic Books, 2018.

Moreton-Robinson, Aileen. *The White Possessive: Property, Power, and Indigenous Sovereignty*. Minneapolis: University of Minnesota Press, 2015.

Murphyao, Amanda, and Kelly Black. "Unsettling Settler Belonging: (Re)Naming and Territory Making in the Pacific Northwest." *American Review of Canadian Studies* 45, no. 3 (2015): 315–331.

Nā Kiaʻi o ka Pō. "Na Wanana i Hooko Ia." *Ke Aloha Aina*. February 27, 1897.

Nā Kiaʻi o ke Ao. "Ahea La Pau Ke Kuhihewa o Ka Lahui." *Ka Nupepa Kuokoa*. March 12, 1897.

———. "Ahea La Pau Ke Kuhihewa o Ka Lahui (Helu 2)." *Ka Nupepa Kuokoa*. March 19, 1897.

Nakaa, G. W. "He Moolelo Hawaii: Olelo Hoakaka." *Ka Nupepa Kuokoa*. January 28, 1893.

Naʻputi, Tiara R., and Michael Lujan Bevacqua. "Militarization and Resistance from Guåhan: Protecting and Defending Pågat." *American Quarterly* 67, no. 3 (2015): 837–858.

Narayan, Kirin. "How Native Is a 'Native' Anthropologist?" *American Anthropologist* 95, no. 3 (1993): 671–686.

Newcomb, Steven. *Pagans in the Promised Land: Decoding the Doctrine of Christian Discovery*. Golden, CO: Fulcrum Publishing, 2008.

Ngata, Tina. "Why I Won't Give the Cook Celebrations My Brown-Ness." *Non-Plastic Maori* (blog), June 2, 2019. https://thenonplasticmaori.wordpress.com.

Niheu, Kalamaokaʻaina. "Puʻuhonua: Sanctuary and Struggle at Mākua." In *A Nation Rising: Hawaiian Movements for Life, Land, and Sovereignty*, edited by Noelani Goodyear-Kaʻōpua, Ikaika Hussey, and Erin Kahunawaikaʻala Wright, 161–179. Durham, NC: Duke University Press, 2014.

Nogelmeier, Puakea, ed. *He Lei No ʻEmalani: Chants for Queen Emma Kaleleonālani*. Honolulu: Bishop Museum Press, 2011.

———. *Mai Paʻa i Ka Leo: Historical Voice in Hawaiian Primary Sources, Looking Forward and Listening Back*. Honolulu: Bishop Museum Press, 2010.

Obeyesekere, Gananath. *The Apotheosis of Captain Cook, European Mythmaking in the Pacific*. Princeton, NJ: Princeton University Press, 1992.

Oliveira, Katrina-Ann R. Kapāʻanaokalāokeola Nākoa. *Ancestral Places: Understanding Kanaka Geographies.* Corvallis: Oregon State University Press, 2014.

Osorio, Jonathan Kamakawiwoʻole. "Hawaiian Souls: The Movement to Stop the U.S. Military Bombing of Kahoʻolawe." In *A Nation Rising: Hawaiian Movements for Life, Land, and Sovereignty,* edited by Noelani Goodyear-Kaʻōpua, Ikaika Hussey, and Erin Kahunawaikaʻala Wright, 137–160. Durham, NC: Duke University Press, 2014.

———. "On Being Hawaiian." *Hūlili: Multidisciplinary Research on Hawaiian Well-Being* 3, no. 1 (2006): 19–26.

Peralto, Leon Noʻeau. "Mauna a Wākea: Hānau Ka Mauna, the Piko of Our Ea." In *A Nation Rising: Hawaiian Movements for Life, Land, and Soverignty,* edited by Noelani Goodyear-Kaʻōpua, Ikaika Hussey, and Erin Kahunawaikaʻala Wright, 232–243. Durham, NC: Duke University Press, 2014.

Pilago, Angel. Interview with the author, December 19, 2013, Kona, Hawaiʻi.

Poepoe, Joseph. "He Moolelo No Kamehameha I: Ka Nai Aupuni o Hawaii." *Ka Nai Aupuni.* October 12, 1906.

———. "Ka Moolelo Hawaii Kahiko: Mokuna I: Na Kuauhau Kahiko e Hoike Ana i Na Kumu i Loaa Ai Ka Pae Moku o Hawaii Nei." *Ka Naʼi Aupuni.* February 2, 1906.

———. "Ka Moolelo Hawaii Kahiko: Mokuna I: Na Kuauhau Kahiko e Hoike Ana i Na Kumu i Loaa Ai Ka Pae Moku o Hawaii Nei." *Ka Naʼi Aupuni.* February 7, 1906.

———. "Moolelo Hawaii Kahiko: Mokuna III: Ka Moolelo o Ko Wakea Ma Noho Ana Ma Kalihi—Ka Loaa Ana o Ke Akua Ula o Kamehaʼikana." *Ka Naʼi Aupuni.* June 21, 1906, 17 edition.

———. "Moolelo Hawaii Kahiko: Mokuna III: Ka Moolelo o Ko Wakea Ma Noho Ana Ma Kalihi—Ka Loaa Ana o Ke Akua Ulu o Kamehaʻikana." *Ka Naʼi Aupuni.* June 26, 1906.

Powell, Emma. "Te ʻAkapapa Nei Tātou: Articulation Theory, ʻAkapapaʻanga and Naming the Cook Islands." Paper presented at the Native American and Indigenous Studies Association Conference, Auckland, New Zealand, 2019.

Pukui, Mary Kawena. *ʻŌlelo Noʻeau: Hawaiian Proverbs and Poetical Sayings.* Honolulu: Bishop Museum Press, 1983.

Pukui, Mary Kawena, and Samuel H. Elbert. *Hawaiian Dictionary: Hawaiian-English, English-Hawaiian.* Honolulu: University of Hawaiʻi Press, 1986.

Pukui, Mary Kawena, E. W. Haertig, and Catherine Lee. *Nānā i Ke Kumu: Look to the Source.* Vol. 2. Honolulu: Hui Hānai, 1972.

Pukui, Mary Kawena, and E. S. Craighill Handy. *The Polynesian Family System in Kaʻū, Hawaiʻi.* Honolulu: Mutual Publishing, 1998.

Purakayastha, Anindya Sekhar. "Eco-Incarceration or Chronicling the Dissidence of Bare Life?" *Economic and Political Weekly* 47, nos. 26 and 27 (June 30, 2012): 256–257.

Qolouvaki, Tagi. "The Mana of Wansolwara: Oceanic Art/Story as Protest and Decolonial Imagining." *Ke Kaupu Hehi Ale* (blog), April 27, 2015. https://hehiale.wordpress.com.

Ranford, Chloe. "Human Rights Advocate Takes Cook Concerns to United Nations." *Stuff,* June 19, 2018. https://www.stuff.co.nz.

Recollect, Karyn. "Gesturing Indigenous Futurities through the Remix." *Dance Research Journal* 48, no. 1 (2016): 91–105.

Republic of the Marshall Islands. "Tile Til Eo: 2050 Climate Strategy 'Lighting the Way.'" September 2018. https://www4.unfccc.int.

Rifkin, Mark. *Beyond Settler Time: Temporal Sovereignty and Indigenous Self-Determination*. Durham, NC: Duke University Press, 2017.

RNZ. "Pacific Scholars Want the Name Moana to Replace Oceania." RNZ, June 27, 2019. https://www.rnz.co.nz.

———. "World's Indigenous People Gather in New Zealand." *Scoop Independent News: Top Scoops*, June 26, 2019. http://www.scoop.co.nz.

Rohrer, Judy. *Staking Claim: Settler Colonialism and Racialization in Hawai'i*. Tucson: University of Arizona Press, 2016.

Rovoi, Christine. "Renaming Oceania: PNG Artist Not Sold on Moana." RNZ, July 4, 2019. https://www.rnz.co.nz.

Rowse, Tim. "Indigenous Heterogeneity." *Australian Historical Studies* 45, no. 3 (2014): 297–310.

S. "He Wanana." *Ka Hae Hawaii*. May 23, 1860.

Sahlins, Marshall. *How "Natives" Think about Captain Cook, for Example*. Chicago: University of Chicago Press, 1995.

Sai, David Keanu. "The American Occupation of the Hawaiian Kingdom: Beginning the Transition from Occupied to Restored State." PhD diss., University of Hawai'i, 2008.

Said, Edward. *Representations of the Intellectual: The 1993 Reith Lectures*. New York: Vintage Books, 1996.

Salesa, Toeolesulusulu Damon Ieremia. "When the Waters Met: Some Shared Histories of Christianity and Ancestral Samoan Spirituality." In *Whispers and Vanities: Samoan Indigenous Knowledge and Religion*, edited by Tamasailau M. Suaalii-Sauni, Maualaivao Albert Wendt, Vitolia Mo'a, Naomi Fuamatu, Upolu Luma Va'ai, Reina Whaitiri, and Stephen L. Filipo, 143–158. Wellington: Huia Publishers, 2014.

Santos Perez, Craig. "Blue-Washing the Colonization and Militarization of Our Ocean: How U.S. Marine National Monuments Protect Environmentally Hamrful U.S. Military Bases throughout the Pacific and the World." *Hawaii Independent*, June 26, 2014. http://www.wrongkindofgreen.org.

Silva, Noenoe K. *Aloha Betrayed: Native Hawaiian Resistance to American Colonialism*. Durham, NC: Duke University Press, 2004.

———. "E Lawe i Ke Ō: An Analysis of Joseph Mokuohai Poepoe's Account of Pele Calling the Winds." *Hūlili: Multidisciplinary Research on Hawaiian Well-Being* 6 (2010): 237–266.

———. "I Kū Mau Mau: How Kānaka Maoli Tried to Sustain National Identity within the United States Political System." *American Studies* 45, no. 3 (2004): 9–31.

———. "Ke Mau Nei Nō Ke Ea O Ka 'Āina I Ka Pono." *Abusalble Past*, August 14, 2019. https://www.radicalhistoryreview.org.

Sissons, Jeffrey. *First Peoples: Indigenous Cultures and Their Futures*. London: Reaktion Books, 2005.

Smith, Jo. "Post-Cultural Hospitality: Settler-Native-Migrant Encounters." *ARENA Journal* 28 (2007): 65–86.

Smith, Linda Tuhiwai. *Decolonizing Methodologies: Research and Indigenous Peoples.* Dunedin, NZ: University of Otago Press, 1999.

State of Hawai'i Department of the Attorney General. "Final Report of the Compacts of Free Association Task Force." 2007. http://ag.hawaii.gov/wp-content/uploads/2013/01/cofa.pdf.

Stephenson, Barry. "On Being 'Close to Nature.'" *Time and Mind: The Journal of Archaeology, Consciousness and Culture* 5, no. 1 (2012): 19–32.

Te Punga Somerville, Alice. *Once Were Pacific: Māori Connections to Oceania.* Minneapolis: University of Minnesota Press, 2012.

———. "Two Hundred and Fifty Ways to Start an Essay about Captain Cook." *New Zealand Journal of History* 53, no. 1 (2019): 3–49.

Teaiwa, Teresia. "For or before an Asia-Pacific Studies Agenda?: Specifying Pacific Studies." In *Remaking Area Studies: Teaching and Learning across Asia and the Pacific,* edited by Terence Wesley-Smith and Jon Goss, 110–124. Honolulu: University of Hawai'i Press, 2010.

Teaiwa, Teresia, and Tekura Moeka'a. "Comparative History in Polynesia: Some Challenges of Studying the Past in the Postcolonial Present." In *Postcolonial Past and Present: Negotiating Literary and Cultural Geographies,* edited by Anne Collett and Leigh Dale, 196–214. Leiden: Koninklijke Brill, 2018.

Tengan, Ty P. Kāwika. "Ka Ulu Koa Ma Kai: The Koa Grove Rises in the Sea." *Pacific Studies* 41, no. 3 (2018): 134–146.

———. *Native Men Remade: Gender and Nation in Contemporary Hawai'i.* Durham, NC: Duke University Press, 2008.

Teves, Stephanie Nohelani. *Defiant Indigeneity: The Politics of Hawaiian Performance.* Chapel Hill: University of North Carolina Press, 2018.

Thiong'o, Ngũgĩ. *Decolonising the Mind: The Politics of Language in African Literature.* Portsmouth, NH: Heinemann, 1986.

Tobin, Jeffrey. "Cultural Construction and Native Nationalism: Report from the Hawaiian Front." *Boundary 2* 21, no. 1 (1994): 111–133.

Trask, Haunani-Kay. "The Birth of the Modern Hawaiian Movement: Kalama Valley, O'ahu." *Hawaiian Journal of History* 21 (1987): 126–153.

———. *From a Native Daughter: Colonialism and Sovereignty in Hawai'i.* Honolulu: University of Hawai'i Press, 1993.

———. "Natives and Anthropologists: The Colonial Struggle." *Contemporary Pacific* 3, no. 1 (1991): 145–177.

Trask, Mililani B. "Hawaiian Sovereignty." *Cultural Survival Quarterly,* March 2000. https://www.culturalsurvival.org.

Tregear, Edward. *Māori-Polynesian Comparative Dictionary.* Honolulu: 'Ai Pōhaku Press, 2014.

Tuan, Yi-Fu. *Topophilia: A Study of Environmental Perceptions, Attitudes, and Values.* Morningside ed. New York: Columbia University Press, 1990.

TVNZ. "Movement to Boycott This Year's 250th Anniversary of Captain James Cook's Landing Gains Strength." TVNZ, May 9, 2019. https://www.tvnz.co.nz.

United Nations. "The United Nations Declaration on the Rights of Indigenous Peoples: A Manual for National Human Rights Institutions." Asia Pacific Forum of National Human Rights Institutions, 2013.

Valeri, Valerio. *Kingship and Sacrifice: Ritual and Society in Ancient Hawaii.* Translated by Paula Wissing. Chicago: University of Chicago Press, 1985.

Veracini, Lorenzo. "On Settlerness." *Borderlands* 10, no. 1 (2011): 1–17.

Webb, Michael, and Camellia Webb-Gannon. "Musical Melanesianism: Imagining and Expressing Regional Identity and Solidarity in Popular Song and Video." *Contemporary Pacific* 28, no. 1 (2016): 59–95.

Wendt, Albert. "Towards a New Oceania." *Seaweeds and Constructions* 7 (1976): 71–85.

Wilson-Hokowhitu, Nālani. "He Pukoa Kani 'Āina." *AlterNative: An International Journal of Indigenous Peoples* 8, no. 2 (2012): 137–147.

Wolfe, Patrick. "Settler Colonialism and the Elimination of the Native." *Journal of Genocide Research* 8, no. 4 (2006): 387–409.

Woolf, Amber-Leigh, and Anna Loren. "One Treaty, One Nation Pamphlet 'Racist and Stupid,' but Not Hate Speech—Academic." *Stuff*, April 14, 2019. https://www.stuff.co.nz.

Young, Kanalu. *Rethinking the Native Hawaiian Past.* New York: Garland Publishing, 1998.

Index

Fermantez, Kali, 115n51
Fiji, 6, 64, 112n11
Finney, Ben, 38, 68, 114n31
"Following the Alaloa Kīpapa of our
Ancestors" (Aikau), 63
Fornander, Abraham, 114n31
French Polynesia, 38. *See also* Tahiti
futurities, 52–55, 62–63, 67, 78–79, 97–99,
103–104. *See also* canoe renaissance;
decolonization; radical hope; space and
time; temporalities; wānana

genealogies, 6–8, 24–29, 101–102, 114n19.
See also Kahiki; kūpuna; mele (chants);
migration
genocide, 88. *See also* West Papua
Goodyear-Ka'ōpua, Noelani, 11, 44–45, 74
Grace, Charlie, 71, 76
Gray, Julia Mage'au, 48
Guåhan (Guam), 42, 64, 105, 122n31
Guardians of the Light, 60–61
Guardians of the Night, 59–60

hale (term), 65
Hale Kūkia'imauna, 65–66, 67, 68, 73
Handler, Richard, 118n7
Handy, E. S. Craighill, 113n29
Harjo, Laura, 52, 54, 62
Harry, Debra, 81, 83–84
Haunui (canoe), 121n36
Hau'ofa, Epeli, 13; on historical
understandings, 61–62; on
homogeneity, 24; "Our Sea of Islands,"
47, 112n7; on world enlargement, 40, 41
Hawaiian Creole English, 119n36
Hawaiian Nation (Lāhui Hawai'i), 12–13
Hawaiian Renaissance, 11, 17, 26, 66–67.
See also activism; agency; canoe
renaissance
Hawaiian sovereignty movement, 7, 12, 26,
66–67. *See also* activism
Hawaiian studies, as discipline, 5. *See
also* Native American and Indigenous
Studies Association (NAISA); Pacific
studies, as discipline
Hawaiian Unity and Liberation Institute
(HULI), 8
Hawai'iloa, 38–39
Hawai'i Tribune-Herald (publication), 99
Hawaiki, 6, 25, 112n11

"He Kanaenae no ka Hanau ana o
Kauikeaouli" (birth chant), 25
Henderson, Tee and Kara, 65
hiki (term), 42
historical agency, 17, 52, 55–57, 59, 62
Hofmeyr, Isabel, 59
Hofschneider, Anita, 31
Hōkūle'a (canoe), 68–69, 118n18
homeland, 6, 112n11. *See also* Kahiki; place,
exercise on
ho'ohiolo, 55–56
ho'omanawanui, ku'ualoha, 115n42
host-guest model, 87–88
Howe, Kerry, 92, 93
Howkins, Adrian, 89
hula, 5, 109. *See also* mele (chants)

Ige, David, 9, 79, 106, 107
Ihumātao, 9–10, 19, 36, 42–45, 80–81. *See
also* Aotearoa/New Zealand; Māori
imagined communities, 12–13
Indigeneity: authenticity and, 66, 67, 118n7;
"closeness to nature" and, 19–20, 22–24,
29; futurities of, 52–55, 62–63, 67,
78–79, 97–99, 103–104; othering and,
85–88; persistent indigeneity, 13, 46, 85;
space and time in, 89, 98–99, 100–103;
trans-Indigeneity, 44–47; unsettling
and, 83–85
Indigenous (term), 19, 45–46, 48, 112n5
"Indigenous Heterogeneity" (Johnson and
Rowse), 88
Indigenous studies, as discipline, 5. *See
also* Native American and Indigenous
Studies Association (NAISA); Pacific
studies, as discipline
interconnectedness, 29–33. *See also* Kahiki;
relationships
internal colonialism, 93–94

Jackson, Moana, 91, 120n23
Japanese laborers, 86–87
Jetnil-Kijiner, Kathy, 112n17
Johnson, Miranda, 88
Jolly, Margaret, 114n25
Justice, Daniel Heath, 87

ka (term), 42
Ka'ahumanu, 39–40
Kabutaulaka, Tarcisius, 48

About the Author

Emalani Case is a Kanaka Maoli lecturer in Pacific studies at Te Herenga Waka–Victoria University of Wellington, New Zealand. She is the author of the blog *He Wahī Pa'akai: A Package of Salt*, which highlights indigenous stories, issues, perspectives, and hopes for the future. She comes from Waimea, Hawai'i.